"The Synergy Strategic Planning process was clear, concise, to the point, and easy to implement. It powered up our management team with a clearer vision, revitalized our values, and put everyone on the same page. It was awesome!! If you want to clearly define your mission and move toward success with confidence, this book is the perfect guide. It's easy to read, and it's full of great examples. Get it today!"

Jeffrey Pitzer, Executive Vice President, GreenLife Solar

"The Strategic Planning Retreat was powerful, and eye-opening. It educated my team to think strategically and that helped us to clarify our vision, understand the importance of our core values, and focus on the main financial drivers of our business. It was a turning point for us."

Erika De La Fuente, Winkir Corporation

"This book is an exceptional guide that will help any business achieve clarity and focus. It is detailed, to the point, and well written. I highly recommend it."

Glenn Noreen, Barrack Obama Charter School

"The Strategic Planning Retreat was a turning point for us. We have grown even in a tough market by using the steps in the program. We are in new markets abroad and nationally. I strongly recommend this book and program."

Lisa Klang, President, Klang and Associates

"Alexander's Synergy program has been an outstanding success for ISI. The Synergy Strategic Planning Retreat brought our entire team on the same page. Our leadership team is still highly motivated, and we achieved several of our business goals using the Synergy tools and models. This book is an outstanding reference guide for management groups. I highly recommend it!"

Scott Grugel, Divisional President, Interior Specialists, Inc.

Choosing to build a high-performance team means you have to love the idea of winning through people.

It requires learning how to lead, coach, nurture, and discipline a team of super achievers focused on a shared destiny.

The results will astonish you!

CHRIS ALEXANDER

SYNERGY

Strategic Planning

A Blueprint for

Organizational Planning

and Execution

Publisher: 1+1=3 Publishing
www.SynergyTeamPower.com
First Edition
Library of Congress Cataloging in Publication Data
Alexander, Chris
Synergy Strategic Planning: A Blueprint for Organizational Planning and Execution
Includes biographical references and index.

Project credits:
    Creative Development: Allen Taylor
    Line Editing: Dale Harvey
    Graphics: Shand Coetzee
    Final Editing: Sharon Young
    Cover, Layout, and Design: Maryna Coetzee

Special thanks to:
    Cynthia Scott, Jim Haines, and Glenn Noreen

Also by Chris Alexander:

Business Books, CDs, and DVDs:
  Synergy Team Power
  The "WOW" Factor!
  The "WOW" Factor! CD
  The "WOW" Factor! DVD
  Synergy Sales Power
  Synergy Leadership
  Joy in the Workplace
  Joy in the Workplace CD Album
  Joy in the Workplace DVD
  Synergizing Your Business Handbook
  Success Is Fun Audio Album
  Synergizing Your Business Audio Album

Personal Development:
  Creating Extraordinary Joy
  Creating Extraordinary Joy CD Album
  Creating Extraordinary Joy DVD
  Synergy Life Mastery Audio Album
  Catch the Wind with Your Wings

If you fail to plan,
you plan to fail.

Contents

*Good fortune is what happens
when opportunity meets with
planning.*

THOMAS EDISON

Foreword

Strategic Planning is like the old-fashioned art of cartography, the making of maps. "Back in your day, Dad," as my sons kiddingly say, "if one wanted to know where to go, you pulled out a map to determine a path to follow. Today, we simply push a GPS button and like lemmings, follow the voice."

Businesses don't have GPS systems to chart their way through treacherous waters toward their goals. Instead of traditional maps, senior executive teams are using synergistic information tools, environmental scanning, intuition, and experience to determine a course to follow. Good CEOs rarely make business decisions about the direction of their companies independently. They normally choose a collaborative, synergistic process.

Synergy Strategic Planning was written to demonstrate how to work as a high-performance team toward a shared destiny. It gives a business leader the insight and methods to create success through Synergy. I have experienced, firsthand, Traditional Strategic Planning, and it's like carving in stone compared to Synergy Strategic Planning. Night and day differences make the task of business planning and execution so much easier, more logical, and much more worthwhile through the Synergy Process. Its foundational principles include committed focused leadership, high-performance teamwork, clear communication, accountability, trust, and belief. These are among the basic tenets of how successful businesses become world-class.

Chris Alexander is an authority on organizational transformation. He is an expert at building high-performance team cultures and is a powerful resource for business consulting, particularly in helping businesses chart their way through the unpredictable, murky, and often choppy waters of today's business challenges.

Based on the success I've experienced with the Synergy Strategic Planning Process, my recommendation to you and your team is to read this book from cover to cover, implement it, and put the principles to the test. The Synergy Strategies produce better financial results and help organizations transition through tough economic times. This distinct competitive advantage will not only move you and your team well into the next up-cycle, but also creates the potential to be at the top of the next wave.

We can do one of two things with excellent information: We can use it or we can lose it. If we use it, we can create something special, a success that is uniquely ours.

REG HARVEY, FORMER CHAIRMAN OF THE BOARD,
VTN SOUTHWEST

Mastering the Context

"I have a serious problem. My productivity is down, customers are complaining about quality, and the staff morale is at an all-time low. I told my guys, 'If you don't turn things around, I'll get someone in here who will.'"

"Eric, it sounds to me as though you're the problem."

"What do you mean, I'm the problem?"

"Eric, your employees tell me they are afraid of you."

"Fear can be a good thing. It keeps them on their toes."

"Fear-motivation does work, Eric, but not very well. It never lasts and you don't get the best out of people, particularly if you continually shout and threaten them with their jobs."

"I don't do that!" Eric shouted, acting out the very thing he just denied.

"Not consciously," I said empathetically. "But there are things that you do that cause people to fear you."

"What things . . . ?"

"Like saying, 'If you want to keep your job, you better not mess up this order.'"

"Chris, my business is not big enough to absorb costly mistakes. I have to make sure that everything runs perfectly."

"Eric, seeking perfection rather than excellence can be extremely stressful for you and your team."

"Tell me about it," said Eric.

After an awkward moment of silence, Eric asked, "What needs to be done, and what do I have to do?"

"Great! We need to start with you. You will need to shift your thinking, which isn't easy. See yourself as a well-seasoned coach taking over a team that needs rebuilding and training, and you want to get them into a championship playoff."

"That's what I've always wanted!"

"Good! You have to help your team learn to be a team. Allow your guys to learn from their mistakes. Mistakes are critical coaching platforms that continuously reduce margins of error. Learning from mistakes boosts confidence and ability, and the team is strengthened—all within a positive guided environment. We need to convert your stressed-out employees into a synergized team of focused go-getters willing to work with you toward a shared destiny."

"Okay, how do we get started?" he asked.

"You begin by sharing your vision with them. What success looks like to you. What you want and how they can be a part of it. Then we will ask them to create their own vision as it relates to their department and specific job. We want the entire team to see themselves being successful in their jobs. We will then meld their collective visions with yours, into one, by conducting a bottom-up, company-wide vision exercise. The feedback from this exercise will be revealing and highly motivational. The goal is to achieve a psychology of shared destiny."

Many CEOs, presidents, and business owners find themselves in similar situations as Eric. It's as if they are stuck in a state of stressful inertia: repeating the same mistakes over and over and not knowing how to become unstuck.

The Synergy Strategic Planning Model is a transformational force that shifts thinking and releases stuck brainpower and energy. It moves an organization away from inertia, lethargy, sameness, and the "blame game," to motivation, growth, and profitability.

Be ruthless with time and gracious with people!

Synergy Strategic Planning

The difference between Traditional Strategic Planning and Synergy Strategic Planning is within the depth and breadth of the managerial leadership focus. In Traditional Strategic Planning, the process is completed at the top by the executive team. It is then committed to writing and, in some cases, word-smithed by an advertising agency and then distributed down into the organization with orders to make the change happen.

In the Synergy Strategic Planning Model, the core principle is that organizational effectiveness is achieved through committed leaders who see the organization as a whole, and that change happens quickly through empowered individuals working in teams toward a shared destiny.

When companies decide to make change, they often overlook the important and vital ingredient that will make all the difference—involving their people in the process! They make the mistake of thinking that everyone will see the benefit of the change. They assume that everyone's goals, aims, and wishes are aligned toward the mission. If you have ever experienced a merger gone wrong or been through any kind of organizational change, you would have undoubtedly experienced the resistance that many people have to change.

You cannot order change, like you order a pizza. Just because the board of directors says it should be so, does not mean that it will be so. Ordering change may work for some people but not for the majority. Making successful change happen in organizations requires a critical mass of agreement and support. That's one of the key reasons and benefits of Synergy Strategic Planning.

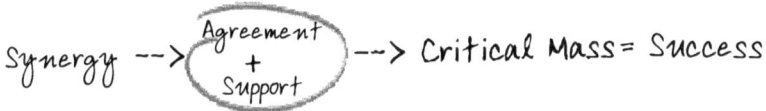

Synergy --> (Agreement + Support) --> Critical Mass = Success

Synergy Strategic Planning is a process of defining a company's mission, vision, and goals. It includes determining a set of core values, which strengthens the relationships between the leadership team, employees, customers, and suppliers. It is a blueprint of the way in which it chooses to do business. It acts as a business's moral compass.

Synergy Strategic Planning requires clarity of thought in determining the key factors for the success of a business by knowing and acknowledging its strengths and weaknesses, what opportunities exist, and what may be a threat to achieving success. It takes into consideration core competencies and core offerings, and is a business discipline that calls for strength of leadership, high-performance teamwork, and unshakable determined focus. *There is nothing more powerful than a passionate team of people, willingly aligning their goals with the company mission and working toward a shared destiny. It is the energy source of success.*

A Psychology of Shared Destiny

A psychology of shared destiny is a power source for growth and profitability. It is a leadership duty and management responsibility to inspire and empower everyone to share in a common vision, a clear set of values, and clearly defined goals. This can be a very difficult thing to accomplish because many leaders are stuck with a false idea of power and control. False power and control can be very intoxicating and hard to let go of because it's good to be king! To be feared! This way of being the king feeds the ego, the imagined self, and creates an illusion of power.

It takes a real shift in thinking and it takes strength of character and personal confidence in one's own ability to recognize that true leadership power is *earned through honesty, competency, trust, and respect.* You cannot lead others if you cannot lead yourself. You have to trust yourself enough to trust others, and in so doing, allow them to perform to their highest potential. This is a more noble way to be king! People love to work for and support secure leaders, and be a part of high energy organizations that afford them the opportunity to grow and develop.

Shared destiny is an essential piece of the success puzzle and a powerful financial engine. Trust between the executive team and the rest of the organization is without question one of the key ingredients to company-wide ownership of the mission.

Most people will not align themselves with bad business practices, executive greed, exploitation, verbal and emotional abuse, betrayal, and false promises. Avoid the mistake of thinking that employees will support any of these unethical practices under the disguise of being a team player.

Most people can read between the lines; they share thoughts, assumptions, and information at the speed of the Internet. In today's businesses, good, bad, assumed, and created news travels really fast. That's why constant and transparent information sharing is critical and vital to organizational change. Facilitating change should follow a set of ethical principles to build a bridge of trustworthiness for employees to walk over without fear.

Experienced consultants and "outside" change agents are invaluable, well-versed, and specialists in rapidly and successfully winning over the hearts and minds of a team. Change agents don't want to captain the ship, they want to "pilot" it out of the harbor. A good captain of business recognizes and uses this talent to cost effectively move the organization forward, knowing that failing to prepare is preparing to fail.

A good leader knows that the difference between a high-performance team and a group of people lies in the following: the strength of the relationships, the work environment, the importance of the goal, and the personal and financial rewards. In a high-performance business team, these factors are stronger, more positive, and applied more often—resulting in increased productivity, reduced costs, and elevated revenues.

You Are in the Business of Directing Energy

A *vision* is a clearly-defined mind image of what the final picture of success looks like. It is a uniquely human ability to imagine and visualize in detail where we plan to end up. To visualize is the most powerful ability we have. When we focus on a specific vision, and we discipline ourselves to hold an image constantly, our bodies become energized to bring about the vision's physical materialization. Imagination is the source of possibility and the foundation of probability. It is the playground of potential, where the seeds of greatness are sown and the power of belief begins.

Every day we draw great inspiration from the heroes of imagination who have come from every walk of life. The Wright Brothers, Einstein, Thomas Edison, Nikola Tesla, Alexander Flemming, Alexander Graham Bell, and Henry Ford imagined radios, televisions, telephones, computers, incandescent light bulbs, automobiles, aircrafts, highways, spacecrafts, and the Internet—and like Martin Luther King, most of them were incorrectly told to stop dreaming about the impossible. Yet, their dreams have proved to be more powerful than the impossible.

> *Dreams are __always__ more powerful than the impossible!*

Writing out a vision statement is fine-tuning the imagination and transporting it into the realm of reality. It's realistic dreaming and is an integral part of a strategic plan.

Equally as important as the vision are the supporting values and goals. Core values form the foundation, behavior, and personality of a business. Core values define and guide the business, allowing employees to identify with the larger purpose: what it stands for and who it serves. Values support the way people and teams communicate with one another and how they build organizational culture. When values are chosen wisely and practiced diligently, a climate of trustworthiness is built between management and staff. This inspires willing attitudes and teamwork. A good strategic plan recognizes that a high-performance team culture incorporates these core values, which is a distinct and powerful competitive advantage.

The business world thrives on high energy, enthusiasm, ideas, and innovation. Ideas and innovation are the lifeblood of business—but the execution and achievement of goals, its energy source. Without clearly defined, written-out, step-by-step goals, a business runs out of gas. New products, solutions, concepts, and the best and most well-intentioned plans will fail consistently without accountability and goals.

Uncontrolled and misdirected enthusiasm is dangerous.

Leadership is in the energy business. Enlightened leadership teams are committed to the idea that a good strategic plan and the organizational culture are the primary operational driving forces in a business. This does not discount the importance of good systems and processes. A Synergy Strategic Plan takes into account the entire organization: all the internal and external influencing factors like the culture, people, systems, policies, resources, and leadership ability to succeed. Leadership commitment is an essential piece to the success of any change and improvement process (see Figure 1).

When we treat each other with dignity, respect, and efficiency, we create a culture of cooperative high performance, which ripples out to the customer.

Teamwork

Goals must be clearly defined but allow flexibility to respond to the dynamic forces of the marketplace.

The Synergy Strategic Planning Blueprint

Figure 1. The Synergy Strategic Planning Blueprint.

The four steps are:

Step 1: Creating an internal mission statement.

Step 2: The completion of a SWOT analysis.

Step 3: Determining the execution essentials.

Step 4: What gets measured gets done.

*If one advances confidently in
the direction of his dreams,
one will meet with a success
unexpected in common hours.*

HENRY DAVID THOREAU

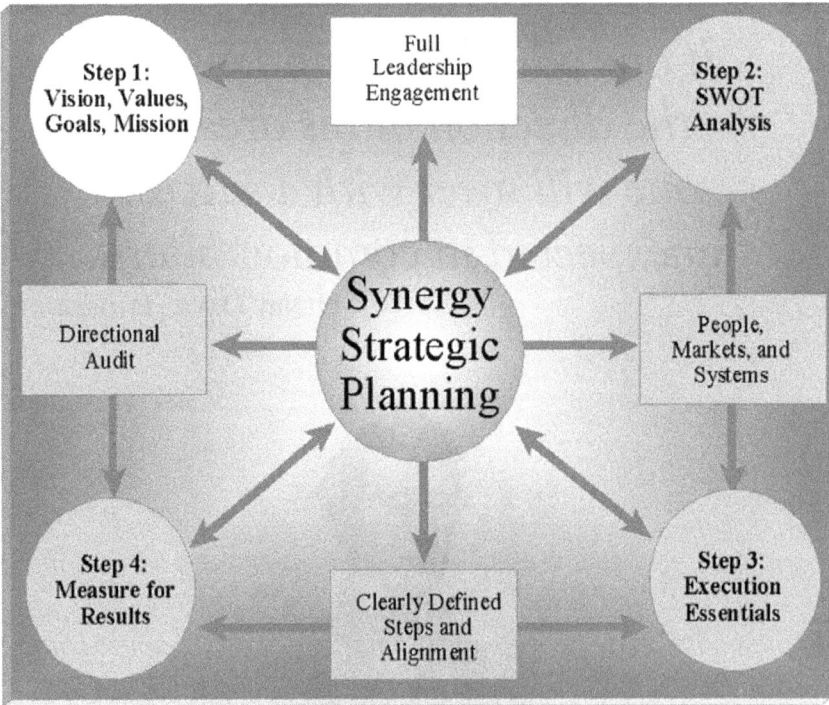

Figure 2. Step 1.

Step One

Creating an Internal Mission Statement, Vision Statement, Core Values, and Goal Plan

The Mission Statement

A mission statement is the constitution of a business. It forms the basis for decision-making and should be a living, breathing part of every workday. This is one of the most valuable steps a leadership team can take and should never be treated lightly. It is often the missing piece in the puzzle of business success.

A clearly communicated mission statement is an energizing phenomenon, a motivational connector. It is the end result of what a good business wants to become. A mission statement must work from the inside out, and it must include the entire team. Your team has to clearly identify with the mission statement. The only way to get a committed buy-in is through involvement and empowerment. That is why you must first begin by constructing an *internal* mission statement.

Don't fall into the trap of having an advertising agency write your mission statement. Many mission statements created by third parties sound good, but don't have a drop of believability and authenticity and therefore lack the emotional engine, which is precisely what is needed to drive motivation and ownership. It must be motivated by the leadership team and be Transformational, Exciting, Authentic, Measurable (TEAM).

The success of the Synergy Strategic Planning Model rests on leadership commitment and a critical mass of high-performance teamwork. Successful implementation requires a broad base of committed ownership.

The exercise below begins with the senior executive team followed by a bottom-up exercise completed in groups of 5-20 (depending on the size of your company). Groups should include divisional presidents, vice presidents, operational managers, department heads, and individuals who are centers of influence. Once the groups have successfully completed the exercise, each group will have a first draft of an internal vision, values, and goals statement. Each group's first draft will be the input into a coordinated final mission statement.

The Exercise

In your respective chosen groups, begin by writing out a vision statement, followed by carefully choosing a clear set of core values and the goals needed to make them a reality. I recommend that each participant begin by writing out a personal vision statement, a personal set of work-related values and broad-based goals and then from the combination of these three, construct a personal mission statement. Personal mission statements should then be shared as input to form a first draft internal vision, values, and goals statement for their group. Further on in this chapter is a series of well-constructed questions provided to assist groups in defining their draft statements. Once each group has concluded this foundational work, construction of a draft mission statement can be completed. A high level of patience is required, and time should be taken to think through each step. A mission statement becomes real or fictitious, depending on whether or not the group can live up to it.

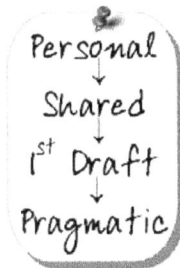

Personal
↓
Shared
↓
1ˢᵗ Draft
↓
Pragmatic

Draft mission statements from all groups are forwarded to and consolidated by a designated mission statement team who then proceeds to construct an overall synergized "shared destiny" internal statement.

After a final review by all participants it can be posted throughout the organization via internal emails, communications, and Intranet. Now the work of company-wide ownership begins. Successful buy-in requires building daily awareness, and a high level of communication is paramount. All education and training should be designed to help employees understand their role in the attainment of the mission. All organizational improvement needs to be supported with measurement, alignment of systems, reward, and reinforcement. As the team progresses and success is achieved internally—and ownership is apparent—an external mission statement can be considered, but don't stray from your core beliefs. Your strength and power is in the authenticity and the integrity of company-wide ownership.

Below are the four strategic steps that form the basis for the construction of an internal mission statement:

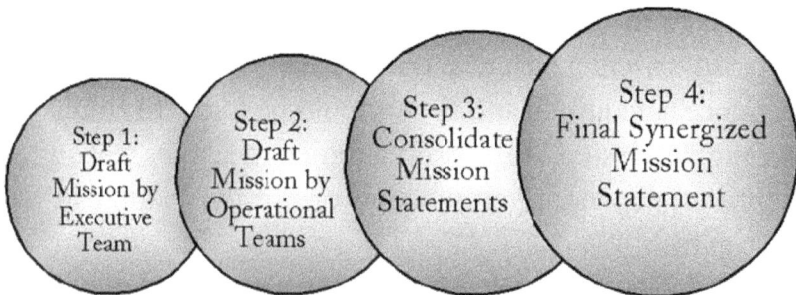

Step 1: Draft Mission by Executive Team

Step 2: Draft Mission by Operational Teams

Step 3: Consolidate Mission Statements

Step 4: Final Synergized Mission Statement

Figure 3. Synergy Internal Mission Steps.

The Vision Statement

A vision statement is a statement about where an organization sees itself within the next five to ten years, taking all its potential for accomplishments into account.

A vision is the dream picture of the business. Henry Ford had a vision of a car in every garage. Steven Jobs had a vision of a computer in every home. John F. Kennedy dreamed of a man on the moon, and Martin Luther King Jr. so eloquently shared his vision through his famous "I have a dream" speech.

To visualize the future and then set up plans to make it a reality is a powerful motivational tool.

Dreamers are the saviors of the Universe.

JAMES ALLEN

Vision Guidelines:
1. Is the vision realistic?

Having dreams and turning them into reality is a major source of human motivation. Dreams give us hope for the future and build possibilities of meaning and fulfillment in our lives. Turning a dream into a clearly-defined vision requires that we think through all the possibilities, probabilities, problems, and potholes that might inhibit its full realization. Working through them in real time is an extremely powerful and liberating process that inspires great passion as the potential for a dream's attainment becomes clearer and more apparent.

Questions that clarify a vision:

1. What business are we in?

2. What business do we want to be in?

3. What will our customers want in the future?

4. Who are our real competitors?

5. What are the external influences that can affect our success?

6. What are the internal influences that can affect our success?

7. Does politics influence our future?

8. What are the financial highroad possibilities?

9. What are the financial low-road possibilities?

10. Do we have a financial resources contingency plan?

2. Does the vision take all possibilities into account?

This question is all-important because it examines all the potential possibilities—both positive and negative—as a prelude to success. To be wise in your planning is of great value. Aristotle Onassis, the shipping magnet and billionaire who married Jackie Kennedy, was considered by many to be wise and prudent in the choices he made. He used a great analytical technique that explored all high- and low-road possibilities. When forecasting, predicting, and planning for success, he would ask his executive team a series of "what-if" questions. First, he would list all the what-if factors in the external environment that might influence the success of the plan. Then, he would turn his team's attention to the internal environment of his business and apply the same technique, asking prudent and searching what-if questions.

What if . . . our product lost its competitive advantage?

What if . . . market variations challenged our current business model?

What if . . . we lost our most loyal customers or employees?

Once this internal and external scanning process was concluded in the planning process, the Onassis team would carefully examine how their strategies, judgments, and decisions would impact the ongoing operational effectiveness. Time after time this method paid off handsomely.

There are many benefits to asking the what-if question. This approach, commonly know as scenario planning, allows a team to predict with some degree of certainty what actions need to be taken if certain events happen. It removes surprise, stress, and anxiety, and helps to rationalize decision-making by anticipating possible changes. It eliminates the rush to judgement that often occurs with unexpected blockages. Change then becomes a source of strength rather than a source of stress.

3. Is the vision a good fit for the culture, leadership, and style of your business?

From time to time, I will work with a company that has a new CEO or has merged with a competitor, and the need for a new and fresh vision is apparent. All too often the leadership team charged with making the change happen smoothly overlooks the need to consider different leadership approaches, cultures, and the differences in the style and pace of each business. Mergers are much more complex than the financial and cost savings synergies might suggest.

Synergizing systems and markets look good on paper but when cultures collide and leadership styles are incompatible—and a go-go business ties up with a slower, more formal structured one—careful planning is required to avoid catastrophe. The most profound vision in the world can be thwarted by insecurity—interpersonal conflict and hardened attitudes that form an underground resistance movement. Cleaning up the people issues is of paramount importance.

Stabilizing leadership styles and creating a unity of command are the keys to the fulfillment of a vision. Systems and structural change are quicker to implement through people-centered change. You can fire everyone and start fresh. You can achieve anything if you have enough money and time, and you are prepared to endure the wrath of shareholders. I would rather plan carefully, communicate effectively, and get people working with me to make the change —it's less expensive and much more effective.

Effective change equals harmony.

4. Is the vision aligned with the values and goals of the organization?

Albert Einstein believed that human beings, to realize their potential, must have clear standards of right and wrong. The most important human endeavor, said Einstein, is striving for morality in our actions.

Morality, said the famous scientist, is what gives beauty and dignity to life. Following our animal instincts is not enough. Without high standards of right and wrong, men cannot live together in peace and friendship.

A business that maintains its integrity—its ethical core—maintains its customers, staff, and profitability. Individual executives and teams should make every effort to work and live in integrity. Integrity, by definition, means an adherence to a code of moral and ethical values—the quality and state of being completely aligned; to be one, to be whole, not separate. Making a prudent choice to connect and be one with a higher path means that our thoughts, values, attitudes, needs, and beliefs must be one with our behavior; to be authentic and trustworthy. This is a tough call. Living in integrity is difficult to even comprehend for those who believe that *the means justify the end.*

Machiaveli had it "easy"!

Choosing alignment and integrating core values in business means making a conscious choice to be transparent; that company policies, procedures, systems, culture, communications, and structure are all congruent and reflected in daily behavior and actions. Integration builds an interlinking, internal strength that will stand the test of time.

That means that all the core values we choose, we live. That we are a product of our own voice, not a game player or a manipulator. It takes inner strength from the senior executive team to stay with what's right and strength to keep to their word. It means honoring commitments. It is the strength to stay away from being deceitful, cheating, stealing, betraying, and speaking with a "forked tongue." It is having an inner resolve that is based on respect and honor for ourselves, others, and the way business should be conducted.

In the final analysis, we are judged on the lasting differences we leave behind. To make a positive difference that echoes down through time clearly takes a higher path of doing business.

5. Does the vision allow for an ever-growing and changing world?

In 1960, 50% of the work force was involved in manufacturing—making things. By the year 2000, only 15% were involved in making things and 66% were in the service sector. Does your business allow for these kinds of changes? Since 1983, U.S. commerce and industry has added more than 100 million computers. Mobile phone subscribers jumped from zero in 1983 to 200 million in 2006. Technology is radically changing the speed and direction of work flow and communication. The housing boom and bust, the credit crunch, the price of oil—all play a major role in running a successful business. The vision must remain dynamic and flexible to survive changing world realities.

6. Does the vision take all the organization's potential for accomplishment into account?

This is a complex question but can be simplified by asking your group: "What would success look like in five to ten years taking all of our potential for accomplishment into account?" A free-flowing and creative debate should form the foundation for this question—allowing "out-of-the-box-thinking." Thoughts and ideas should be listed and revisited, and no area should be excluded. You will be surprised at the hidden desires and subconscious underpinnings that reveal themselves. Following are examples of how well this question works.

Some years ago I conducted a strategic planning retreat for Amylin Biotech Corporation, then headed up by Ted Green and Dr. Tim Rink, who both supported the visionary focus of this question. Interestingly, one of the outcomes from this question, and the lively debate around it, was that the senior executive team—for the first time—reached a meeting of minds that the true vision for Amylin was to become a fully fledged pharmaceutical company, and not a boutique biotech company. This resulted in the renaming of the company to Amylin Pharmaceuticals, Inc. and, in turn, clarified its vision: core values and goals.

Amylin Pharmaceuticals has gone on to become one of San Diego's best places to work and their current mission is as follows:

"Amylin Pharmaceuticals is a biopharmaceutical company committed to improving lives through the discovery, development and commercialization of innovative medicines."

I worked with several companies in the building industry who made significant changes by asking this question. Like Amylin, they reaped enormous benefits in leadership focus, levels of quality, and customer satisfaction, thus reducing costs and increasing revenues. It is common knowledge that the building industry worldwide has undergone enormous transformation. In California, the SB800 Bill (arbitration bill) ratified in the State Assembly in 2003 required homebuilders to improve the quality of their product and services to homebuyers.

When I consulted with these companies and went through the vision guideline questions, it was soon discovered that many internal changes were needed to be in compliance with the SB800 Bill. Because of this, I guided several companies through the process of building customer-driven cultures, which meant that we needed to align systems and processes, and focus all staff on a shared destiny.

The first step was conducting several Synergy Team Power Retreats to lay the foundation for change. All staff members from sales, accounting, construction, customer service, land acquisition, planning and engineering, and the entire senior executive team attended the retreats. To demonstrate commitment to the shared destiny, the senior executive team attended more than one retreat. This formed a foundation of solid communication, willing attitudes, and a productive, transparent work environment— shifting mentality and creating a critical mass of ownership to the shared destiny.

Simultaneously, we conducted a series of strategic planning workshops that went through an initial education step and then a series of workshops that included interactive group dynamic exercises resulting in building a vision statement, a clear set of values, and broader generic goals (e.g., improving quality, customer service, and teamwork). Once each executive team reached this stage and the vision was completed and ratified, it was circulated throughout the company for input and approval. Some changes were made, mostly "word-smithing" in nature, until the vision statement was finally published and distributed.

"We have always been committed to building trust, communication, and respect with our customers and employees. Our customer-care program is a sentiment to our dedication of providing world-class service and helping people to achieve the American dream."

SCOTT GRUGEL, DIVISIONAL PRESIDENT,
INTERIOR SPECIALISTS, INC.

F.W. Woolworth's Ten-Cent Vision

When young F.W. Woolworth was a store clerk, he convinced his boss to support his vision to have a ten-cent sale to reduce inventory. The boss agreed, and the idea was a resounding success.

This inspired Woolworth to open his own store and price items at a nickel and a dime. He needed capital for such a venture, so he asked his boss to supply the capital for part interest in the store.

His boss turned him down flat. "The idea is too risky," he told Woolworth. "There are not enough items to sell for five and ten cents." Woolworth went ahead without his boss's backing, and he not only was successful in his first store, but eventually he owned a chain of F.W. Woolworth stores across the nation. Later, his former boss was heard to remark, "As far as I can figure out, every word I used to turn Woolworth down cost me about a million dollars."

AUTHOR UNKNOWN

7. Is the vision inspiring and uplifting?

I am often asked: "How do I motivate my team—should I give them more money?" Money always helps, but if you make the relationship with your team and what they do for you just about money, then that will be the primary motivator. Your relationship with employees should be about more than just a paycheck. Generation "Y" and for that matter, other generations want a deeper relationship. They want a sense of belonging and a sense of purpose through more meaningful work, recognition, fun, and involvement in the things that affect their jobs and future.

Inspirational leaders and companies inspire their employees with uplifting dream pictures, which ignites one of the true keys to motivation: the possibility and probability of achieving something extraordinarily great—together.

Imagination is the power switch for all potential. It is where a visual image is engineered into a seed of creation—the doorway through which all of us manifest our hopes and dreams, which spark the flames of directed passion and shared destiny.

Imagination is the workshop of the mind. It is where dreams and hopes are connected with a sense of purpose.

When the Disney creative team invented the word "imagineering" for the Epcot Center, they knew just as Walt Disney did that this was where the creative force of great things began: in the engineering of a great vision.

Jim Collins and Jerry Porras, in their book *Building Your Company's Vision,* talked about creating a BHAG—A Big Hairy Audacious Goal.

"A true BHAG is clear and compelling, serves as a unifying focal point of effort, and acts as a clear catalyst for team spirit. It has a clear finish line, so the organization can know when it's achieved its goal. People like to shoot for finish lines."

Companies that create an inspiring and uplifting vision mobilize the energy and focus of their team, and lay a foundation for the creation of a high-performance team culture. It is critical and strategically necessary.

When planning for a year,
plant corn.
When planning for a decade,
plant trees.
When planning for life,
train and educate people.
CHINESE PROVERB

High-Performance Team Culture —A Competitive Advantage

Culture through Inheritance and Environment

Many characteristics and behaviors are acquired from national cultures and passed on from generation to generation. Families also pass down ways of doing things, learned rituals, behaviors, and values. It is traditional to steadfastly preserve culture for fear that it may dilute steadily and ultimately disappear. It is an important part of humanity; it is our way of consistently validating individual identity and maintaining the norms of civilization.

Some of our characteristics and behaviors are genetically inherited, such as certain physical attributes, particular family similarities like voice tone, physical posture, body shape, and so on. We are products of hereditary but we are also products of the environment. Researchers have had a long-standing debate on whether we are products of our hereditary or our environment. My conclusion to this confusing debate is the following:

If you look like Mom and Dad, you are a product of hereditary; but if you look like the next door neighbor, you are a product of the environment.

Culture through Choice

More seriously, we are products of even more than our genetics and environment. We are products of our learned behaviors, shared values, beliefs, philosophies, experiences, habits, expectations, and most importantly, our choices. People inherit culture, accept culture, embrace and practice it, and we can create it by choice.

Culture shock is common to immigrants. Adaptation and adjustments cause stress, anxiety, and frustration. As human beings, we draw our emotional security from our known values, beliefs, and expectations. Changing our ingrained, emotionally-secure ways, habits, and beliefs is not easy to do. For strategic planning purposes and performance improvement, understanding the negative and positive reactions to change is of great importance. Building a strong organizational culture has immense and profound strategic advantages. Once established, strong cultures made up of solid work ethics, respectful communications, and quality workmanship create a consistent, self-monitoring, emotionally secure, high-performance team.

A stable workforce, where the relationships at all levels of the organization are based on agreed values, engenders a willing and greater commitment. Strong cultures have *less* attrition, *less* conflict resolution, *less* politics, and financial exposure. As a general rule, people don't sue people they like. One of the most powerful human motivators is a sense of belonging. When we feel we belong, it is a validation of our existence.

We will go to extraordinary lengths to protect who we are. Our culture helps to explain our identity and gives us our uniqueness, and we will fight to protect it.

Organizational culture is a *synergized* and energized system of:

1. Vision, Values, and Goals

2. Beliefs and Principles

3. Leadership: Philosophy/Style/Commitment

4. Experiences: Successes and Failures

5. Training and Development

6. Systems and Structure

7. Sense of Urgency/Habits

8. Expectations: Leadership and Staff

9. Norms/Standards/Boundaries

10. Behaviors: Formal and Informal

11. Decision-making Process

12. Historical Depth and Inspiration

13. Empowered Problem-solving

14. Organizational Ecology

1. Vision, Values, and Goals

These form the foundation for shared destiny and create the big picture needed to get the entire organization moving together in one direction.

2. Beliefs and Principles

These talk to how you believe your business should be run and held accountable. There are standard principles that are ingrained and acceptable to the larger culture and always work, such as:

- Respect for the individual.

- Respect for the company.

- Honesty—candid open communication and clear transparency.

- Trustworthiness—actions and behaviors that lead to trusting one another. Being truthful and being competent.

- Responsibility—exercising good judgement; disciplined actions and behaviors; making the right choices. *No right thing can come from irresponsible decisions. No wrong thing can come from right responsible decisions.*

- Fair work environment—a more civilized and enlightened workplace that's fair to all.

- Citizenship—a commitment to the company vision, values and goals, and adherence to policies and procedures. Every organization has house parameters and rules, which are important because they clearly set-up expectations and clear, understandable boundaries—but they should not be used to stifle innovation, creativity, suggestions, and opinions.

- Teamwork/Cooperation—help one another break down silos and politics.

3. Leadership: Philosophy/Style/Commitment

What philosophy do you choose to run your business? Consistency of philosophy is vital. Inconsistency and lack of clarity create a lack of confidence, mistrust, and insecurity. Flip-flopping on decisions and not making a clear choice about how you want to run your business and how you believe business should be conducted sends a clear message of incompetence. Whatever your philosophy, make it clear and communicate it. Success comes in many sizes and packages. There is a wealth of information in the companion handbook: *Synergy Leadership*.

Consistently "bad" is sometimes better than the leadership flavor of the week!

4. Experiences: Successes and Failures

Experiences, knowledge, successes, failures, and near misses all play into the system of building a culture of high-performance. The most important of these experiences are the ones in the present: how people experience relationships, atmosphere, communications, and so on. If the experience is in alignment with the leadership talk, trust and respect are built. Environments and work experiences play heavily into job satisfaction, commitment, and longevity.

The messenger is not shot but encouraged to identify possible solutions in "tandem" to problems; emotional "dumping" of problems onto management with no thought of remedies perpetuates the high-blame game.

5. Training and Development

To build a high-performance culture, you need to be ready to educate and focus on training as an investment rather than a cost. Selection is important. You can't always hire the perfect person, but you can develop them when you hire for attitude and train for skills. There is not enough argument for the value of training employees. It should be seen as an integral part of any and all strategic planning. Great sports coaches know that you can't take a team into the locker room once a year for a pep talk and expect them to become national champions. They train their teams every day in every part of the game and in every aspect of life. So, in business, why we think we can throw someone into a job and expect them to succeed, defies all logic. Yet, this is practiced daily. To build a championship team, training needs to be a core value. I have had many debates with senior executives who have had the view that training is an added expenditure and it's acceptable to splurge a little by sending staff on a training seminar, but only when business is good. This is exactly why many businesses in the west are losing ground to global competitors every day. Training is a distinct and major competitive advantage.

Here are a number of the important reasons to invest in executive education and training:

- increases productivity;
- improves performance;
- increases efficiency;
- reduces costs;
- lowers attrition;
- lowers absenteeism;

Training is an investment, not a cost, to the organization and the individual!

- improves motivation;
- enhances job satisfaction;
- improves job enrichment;
- improves quality;
- develops talent;
- prepares for promotion; and
- builds culture and loyalty.

Training must be done correctly because one way or another there is a cost but not necessarily a benefit if it's unplanned via the peer process.

6. Systems and Structure

Organizational systems and structures influence the way employees, customers, and suppliers relate to a company. It is imperative that the systems and structures are aligned with leadership communication and style. For example, if your vision is to exceed customer expectations, but your customers have to jump through hoops to purchase or return a product, your vision will have very little believability with both internal and external customers.

Synergy Strategic Planning is an all-inclusive business approach that focuses on synergizing people, systems, structures, and processes to successfully achieve the mission and specific predetermined goals that drive the financial engine.

7. Sense of Urgency/Habits

Organizational habits are formed by the leadership personality, systems, and processes, and the organizational implementation of positive and negative consequences of choice and actions. The habits of leadership are by far the most influencing factor impacting the responses and actions of the majority of the staff. "It all rolls downhill—never a truer word spoken." Even independent thinkers and individuals who do not compromise themselves easily, still look to their leaders for guidance, input, and direction.

8. Expectations: Leadership and Staff

Living up to and matching or exceeding employee expectations is by far one of the most powerful motivators. Throughout history, the example of demonstrated commitment to goals and the willingness of leadership to work as a high-performance team spurs others on to follow their lead enthusiastically. Making change without communication or not considering the impact of change will manifest stress and lead to unexpected and—unreasonable—unethical behaviors. A lack of communication will break down teamwork, trust, respect, and inevitably lead to the formation of subcultures, dissension, and even sabotage. Think of the many mergers that hoped for financial synergies, but ignored the importance of human synergy—and failed because of it.

Ignoring human synergy is like tossing the pieces of a puzzle on the floor and expecting them to fit together on their own accord!

9. Norms/Standards/Boundaries

What is normal for one company can be unusual for another. Clear communication about the way companies want to relate to staff, suppliers, and customers goes a long way to setting up workable relationship boundaries. Clearly communicated and defined boundaries lead to secure understandings of the way in which a company operates. All too often conflict results from the lack of communication in this area. This is true for every level of the organization, but of paramount importance in operations.

In one company, for example, it would be the norm to challenge the CEO but in another, it would be suicide.

Disney, Southwest Airlines, and many other companies have strategically implemented an induction program for new employees for this very reason. This sets the stage to introduce boundaries, policies, and procedures. It introduces the new employee to the culture and is a platform for re-enforcing expectations and norms, and sets the tone for the overall culture.

10. Behaviors: Formal and Informal

This is probably the most critical area of all. Behaviors are formed and reinforced by organizational culture. Almost all performance issues can be tracked back to culture. Most behaviors in the workplace are a result of the leadership style, how decisions are made, the systems and processes employed, and whether communications are open or closed.

As mentioned at the beginning of this section, people are a product of their learned experiences, shared values, and habits—but the most important is choice. People make prudent choices about how they should behave at work and at large. National cultures, plus present-moment choices and needs, determine behaviors. Choosing and learning effective behavioral skills that assist managers and employees to communicate effectively, reduces conflict and creates a workplace that people love to come to. The key is a commitment by the leadership team to walk the talk—to practice and role model the behaviors and interactions they want to see. Learning to appreciate and deal with different personalities and elevating interpersonal communications with regard to mistakes, errors, and redirecting in a coaching manner, is of immeasurable value. Teamwork values are of great importance, but sustainability is achieved through the senior executive team, visible ownership, and operational management's daily one-on-one interactions with staff.

11. Decision-making Process

Decisions validate the vision, values, and goals. The culture should form a platform for decision-making—even profoundly important financial decisions. The reason we employ people is to advance the organization's productivity and performance; therefore, it fails all measures of common sense not to refer to, and take into account, the impact of decisions on the people and the culture.

Decisions on promotions, bonuses, invitations, vacations, training and development, performance appraisals, and new executive hires need to be communicated effectively.

12. Historical Depth and Inspiration

Individuals are motivated by connecting to the roots of the business. How did the company start? Who were the players? How did the surfer become president? Who was the greatest salesman? What characters helped make up the company's personality? Cultures are made up of history, vision, possibilities, and potential—but hearts and minds are won by

giving the company an attractive personality—
something emotional to fall in love with—a desirous
relationship. The senior executive team forms the
leadership and company personality, and sets the
internal brand loyalty.

13. Empowered Problem-solving

Culture should permeate every nook and cranny
of the business and if teamwork is a value (as it should
be), then live up to that value by empowering
individuals with relevant decision-making in every
department and in every job. One of the most
successful ways to teach people how to make decisions
is to empower and involve them in regular Synergy
Team Power meetings. Synergy Team Power meetings
are all about working creatively, constructively, and
continuously, together and individually, to achieve
concrete key improvements.

Each team member is encouraged to make
decisions and set goals for their specific jobs: to take
complete responsibility and understand their sphere
of influence, and willingly be held accountable to the
team and its progress. Empowered teamwork is a
powerful way to create personal awareness and
growth. Teams learn how jobs are interlinked and
aligned to achieve organizational objectives, and that
what they do is important.

14. Organizational Ecology

Humans psychologically and physiologically respond well to warm, secure, understandable, and agreeable environments. Healthy, honest, supporting, and rewarding communication builds a climate of security. Research has demonstrated that people work best when they are considered, acknowledged, and included. As the pace of life has accelerated, technology, isolation, and distance have impacted our lives. Work relationships have become ever more important. People today are forming friendships and bonds that go beyond normal work relationships. This influences what kind of environment to foster and what new skills need to be learned to lead effectively. It is a distinct, clear, and present opportunity to direct energy and build zones of inspiration and more profitable work environments.

Frederick Herzberg talked about two important factors that need to be in place to create a balanced environment for good workplace performance. He called them hygiene factors and motivational factors. If hygiene factors are not in place, this leads to dissatisfaction and then motivational factors are not effective—but if hygiene factors are in place, motivational factors work and lead to satisfaction.

-**Hygiene factors** are status, job security, salary, fringe benefits, company policies, and supervisory practices.

-**Motivational factors** are challenging work, recognition for performance, responsibility, advancement, and growth.

Herzberg's research was profound and helped managers understand that job enrichment leads to motivation and improved performance.

In their groundbreaking book *Primal Leadership*, Daniel Goleman, Richard Boyatzis, and Annie McKee support Herzberg's research but go further by suggesting that a leader who achieves the best performance from employees is emotionally intelligent, self-aware, self-managed, socially aware, and good at relationship management. Many of the organizations and teams I have worked with have always performed better when the atmosphere and energy were positive. Leadership style and ability are vital to balanced relationships, atmosphere and, in turn, job enrichment and high-performance teamwork.

The greater complexity of business today and the evolution of the workplace suggests that there are more areas in need of consideration. Following are four basic organizational ecology factors (physical, emotional, structural, and synergy) that need to be included.

1. Physical ecology relates to the physical work environment, which needs to be clean, hygienic, and warm, and allow employees to concentrate on

working efficiently and effectively. Will this motivate people to greatness? No, but poor working conditions will certainly "de-motivate" them.

2. Emotional ecology relates to organizational relationships. Relationship management is integral to success. Motivation is an emotion, not a logical process, so make sure disappointments and conflicts are dealt with as soon as possible. Also make sure that relationships are sound and strong, so as to enable your team to bond, grow, develop, and build greater performance. If an organization is filled with emotional turmoil, employees will not stay, no matter how much they are paid.

3. Structural ecology refers to leadership style. In a synergistic structure, people are involved in the decisions that affect them and their families. The structure must allow a free flow of information between all levels of the organization. Horizontal and vertical communication are necessities in today's competitive market. If team players are not informed of changes that directly affect them, they will feel insecure. If you give people a clear vision and a sense of purpose, and discuss the reasons why they benefit, then most employees will bear almost any circumstance to transform the vision into reality.

Create a purpose for those around you. Give them something greater to strive for and let them come to work on purpose.

*Great minds have purpose;
others have wishes.*

WASHINGTON IRVING

4. The synergy ecology refers to pulling it all together by focusing the whole business toward predetermined shared goals. It means understanding the power of directed creativity, commitment, and energy, and using it to create an environment of extraordinary performance.

What's Synergy?

When synergy is at work in your organization, it replaces fear with desire. It builds quality workmanship and a sense of pride in accomplishment through teamwork. It is self-managing and strives for continuous improvement as a natural consequence of its meaning.

Synergy is optimistic. It builds bridges of unity and breaks down walls of triviality. Every step forward and every achievement becomes a gratifying learning process.

Synergy devastates greed and eliminates destructive egos. It powers up innovation and stifles bureaucracy. It allows everyone to say "us" instead of "us and them." It creates a sense of belonging, purpose, and job enrichment.

People are at their best when they interact and cooperate with one another. Heroes are created out of everyone and Triple Win relationships become a way of life, where the employee wins, the company wins, and the customer wins . . . in that order.

Synergy is a force that will work for you; all you have to do is let it.

Triple Win

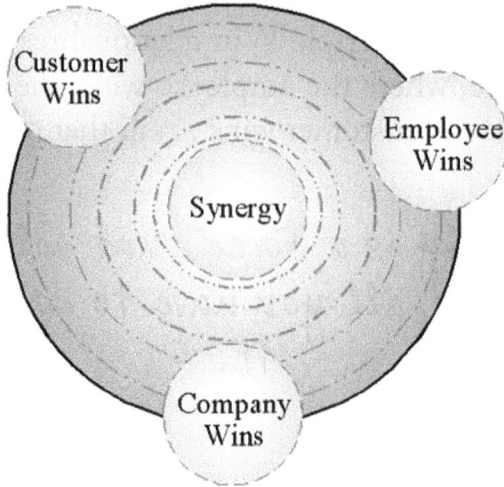

Triple Win is just this: Employees win by working for leaders who are committed to the principle of service. They see themselves improving the quality of their lives through the relationship they have with the company and the work they do. In this way, the employee wins, the company wins, and the customer wins.

It works from the inside out. Employees who are well-trained and empowered and have job satisfaction are more invested in educating and serving the customer who will reward the company with continued loyalty. Building a community of loyal customers in this way is a good reason for seeing your training dollars as an investment rather than an expense and a drain on profits. It's a simple yet powerful way to build a customer-driven culture from the inside out.

Making 1+1=3 or more . . .

Choosing Values

Core values form the foundation of culture. Our beliefs, behaviors, and principles influence the way we communicate with one another. What sits well with us forms a relationship bond that connects each individual to the company, to one another, and to the direction of the organization. Core values define, inform, and guide our businesses. Core values form a platform for decision-making, a guideline for ethical governance, and allows all employees the opportunity to identify with the larger purpose of the business.

Values = Moral Compass = Integrity

Businesses are made up of individuals and their collective moral, ethical, and spiritual agreements, which have a powerful influence on decisions. When a business is transparent, it means that it is straight-lining (no hidden agendas); it is in alignment. What a business *says* it does—and what it *actually* does—are reflections of its integrity. This is how trust-worthiness is built. Values, like a vision, need to permeate every part of the business. Departments and functions need to be integrated and aligned with the larger vision and values. One of the prime demotivators for employees is duplicitous behavior by the leadership team, creating a climate of cognitive dissonance.

Cognitive dissonance is a psychological state that describes the anxiousness felt when behaviors are in conflict with thoughts and beliefs. Organizational dissonance occurs when the company says one thing and does another. The effect of organizational dissonance causes a lack of trust and loyalty.

Transparency, authenticity, and integrity are all from the same family. When a sense of service to one another prevails and is extended out to the customer, trustworthiness is experienced by the customer, making it easier to make decisions to purchase a product or service.

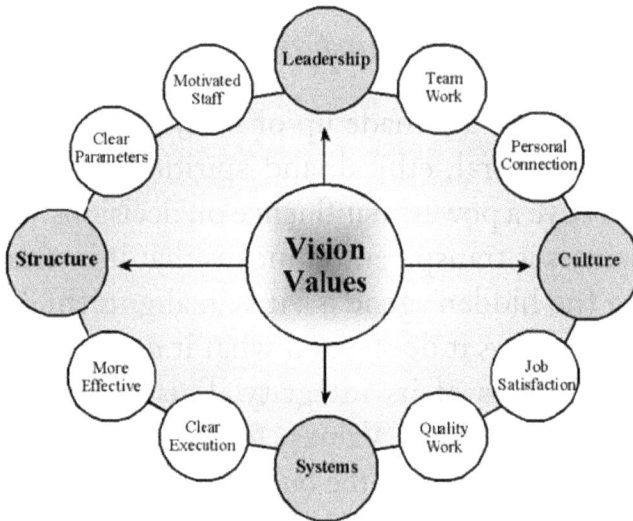

Figure 4. Synergy Values Alignment Model.

The Synergy Values Alignment Model is a proactive process by which the elements of Leadership, Culture, Systems, and Structure are brought into an ethical and sustainable alignment.

Values Must Be Clear and Acceptable

When choosing core values, choose high standards that you can stick to through thick and thin. Firm, fair, but not rigid adherence builds internal security, trust, and confidence in the leadership team. Many daily situations will call for flexibility—but flexibility must be applied to procedures, not to core values. Strong core values and a strong culture help to avoid the pitfalls created by new department heads or divisional presidents who, by changing communications and focus, can destroy overall morale by crushing clear-rooted, acceptable values.

Acceptability of strong core values by the team strengthens organizational responsibility and synergy, which strengthens performance. Integrity is not an option, and the means do not satisfy the end.

The Organization Must Be Able to Live Up to its Values

Well-thought-out and acceptable values make an outstanding contribution to the success of any organization. Living up to a chosen set of core values will always be where the "rubber hits the road." Core values should be strong enough to sustain people even during times of crises.

Discipline and judgement are of paramount importance. Natural greed, impatience with the pace of the markets or economy, and losing focus can take you off-track.

Enron, Worldcom, and the sub-prime mess were due in large part to a lack of discipline and judgement by senior executives—making it up as they went along—substituting integrity with personal greed. These are prime examples of doing what's currently fashionable—look good—project the right image— while having a hidden agenda. This is precisely what makes the general public at large think that all businesses do not deserve to be trusted.

On the other hand, there are organizations that live up to their values and demonstrate through their actions that they are a product *of* their product. These organizations are revered and even loved, creating brand loyalty and communities of customers for life. They are like a fresh cool breeze on a hot, clammy, summer day.

They Must be Clearly Displayed

When I was writing this section, I decided to go on the Internet to see what kind of companies listed their core values for the world to see—and I was surprised by the results of this informal research project.

First listed was Harbor Industries, Inc.—but thereafter it was mainly churches, schools, states, and nonprofit organizations all the way down to #20, The Great Northern Corporation; #25, Cardinal Health; #31, Eriksons; #45, NC Bank; and so on. Upon investigation as to why values were not displayed, the answer I received from several companies was that in a litigious society, it's best not to advertise values because someone could point to them and claim that the company does not live up to its promises. Let me make this clear: If you are a value-driven organization, you do everything to live up to your values, because they form the culture of your organization and must never, *never* be considered as something to be hidden. Companies that are afraid to post their values don't believe in them, or themselves.

Leadership Must be Able to "Walk the Talk"

Companies that openly display their values stand behind them with constant reminders to executives and staff. If a customer is dissatisfied, the values are the very platform a company returns to for evaluation. Value-driven organizations experience a dramatically lower level of lawsuits and dissatisfied customers. The leadership choice is to give everyone clearly defined parameters and confidently move forward by practicing continuous improvement. Of course, when practicing continuous improvement, measurement is all-important, which is covered in Step 4 of this book.

Fraud and Corruption
Stemming the Surge – 04/17/08

A day after warning the Senate about a "tremendous surge" in the FBI's mortgage fraud investigations, Director Robert Mueller talked in more detailed terms about the growth in both corporate fraud and public corruption at the annual conference of the American Bar Association.

Mueller said that the FBI's corporate fraud cases have grown more than 80 percent since 2003. Last year, we had more than 490 corporate and securities fraud convictions.

He said the "ripple effect of the sub-prime crisis and its impact on the credit market will worsen. The FBI has already identified 19 corporate fraud matters related to the sub-prime lending crisis . . . targeting accounting fraud, insider trading, and deceptive sales practices. And, we're currently investigating more than 1,300 mortgage fraud matters."

Mueller believes part of the problem is "rampant conflicts of interest in the corporate suites." He said that FBI investigations, "further emphasize the need for independent board members, auditors, and outside counsel. Shareholders rely on the board of directors to serve as the corporate watchdog . . . (but) board members are often beholden to the executives they are expected to oversee."

PHILOSOPHERS BLOG

The Courage of His Convictions

Abe Lincoln made the greatest speech of his senatorial campaign at Springfield, Illinois.

The convention before which he spoke consisted of a thousand delegates together with the crowd that had gathered with them.

His speech was carefully prepared. Every sentence was guarded and emphatic. It has since become famous as "The Divided House" speech. Before entering the hall where it was to be delivered, he stepped into the office of his law partner, Mr. Herndon, and, locking the door, so that their interview might be private, took his manuscript from his pocket, and read one of the opening sentences: "I believe this government cannot endure permanently, half slave and half free."

Mr. Herndon remarked that the sentiment was true, but suggested that it might not be good policy to utter it at that time.

Mr. Lincoln replied with great firmness: "No matter about the policy. It is true, and the nation is entitled to it. The proposition has been true for six thousand years, and I will deliver it as it is written."

AUTHOR UNKNOWN

Preparing a Values Statement

A values statement is the integrity declaration by the organization of the way it relates to its people, suppliers, and customers. It is the emotional driving force of success. Along with your team, discuss the core values that create a foundation of integrity. Create a critical mass of ownership into building a work environment that creates relationships based on more than just the hourly wage. This is a true source of a motivated workforce.

Under the checklist below, you will notice that quality, customer service, and a fair workplace are all values. It is important to understand and communicate what your values are to internal and external customers. What are the values of your organization?

Choosing Values: Summarized Guidelines

- Values = moral compass = integrity. Values are about the ethics of your business.
- They must be clear and acceptable to your entire team.
- The organization must be able to live up to its values.
- They must be clearly displayed for everyone to see.
- The leadership must be able to "walk the talk."

Values Statement Questions

The following questions will assist your team to clearly understand the importance of values and serve to facilitate in the completion of a values statement.

- Do you have a clear set of agreed values?

- Do you have a clear set of customer values?

- Do you have a clear set of supplier values?

- Do you have a clear set of employee values?

- Do you have a clear set of performance values?

- Do you have a clear set of cultural values?

Business Values Checklist

- Quality of products and services.

- Respect for individuals and company.

- Responsibility in all decisions and actions.

- Responsive to internal and external customers.

- Attention to detail—accuracy—do it right the first time.

- Cleanliness: work areas, restrooms, factories, service areas, and staff.

- Punctuality: work, meetings, creditors, and communications.

- Urgency: Do it now; avoid procrastination.

- Professionalism: behavior, attitude, focus, dress, diligence, and performance.

- Communication: honest, respectful, curious, polite, open, accurate, regular, and complete.

- Synergy: people, systems, and structure focused toward a shared destiny.

- Trust: trustworthy behaviors: management and staff, company and customers, suppliers and company.

- Professional ethics and integrity:
  - accounting practices;
  - human resources;
  - sales and marketing;
  - manufacturing;
  - intellectual property; and
  - interpersonal communication.

- Discipline: personal, policies, schedules, goals, and commitments.

- Accountability: acceptance of and adherence to performance, results, mistakes, etc.

- Integration and alignment: smooth operating systems and alignment—horizontally and vertically—toward organizational priorities (shared destiny).

- Continuous improvement: ongoing constant shaping—changing, growing, and improving.

- The customer: a declaration of your ethics and values.

- Attitude: positive, inspiring, and motivating.

- Innovation: product development, new market ideas, and staying ahead of trends.

- Training and development: a commitment to well-trained management and staff; development of talented individuals; commitment to motivating staff through educational growth; support for training that "WOWs" customers.

- Creativity: brainstorming sessions; open to new ideas.

- Empowerment: a commitment to releasing the brainpower of each individual in the company by allowing them responsibility for solutions and actions.

- Decisiveness: well-timed, well-thought-out decision-making.

- Determination: stick to a plan and not be swayed by the "flavor of the month."

- Fun: Have fun at work—make it an enjoyable environment.

- Loyalty: to company, people, and suppliers.

- Achievement: Value the attainment of goals, budgets, and vision.

- Excellence: Strive for personal and business excellence.

- Joy in the workplace: Build a value-driven culture that focuses on strengths and rewards performance.

- Fair workplace: Build a work environment that is fair to all executives and staff.

- Talent: Respect and reward talented people.

- Leadership: Manage your systems, processes, and cash flow—but lead people.

- Diversity: Respect and focus on the strengths of others to build trust.

- Knowledge: Become a learning organization.

- Environment: Build an exciting, acceptable, and "great" place to work.

- Education: Promote education at all levels for all ages.

- Teamwork: Build a high-performance team spirit by promoting cooperation and collaborative team efforts and projects.

Aunt Karen

A teacher told her young class to ask their parents for a family story with a moral at the end of it, and to return the next day to tell their stories.

In the classroom the next day, Joe gave his example first:

"My dad is a farmer and we have chickens. One day we were taking lots of eggs to market in a basket on the front seat of the truck when we hit a big bump in the road; the basket fell off the seat and all the eggs broke. The moral of the story is not to put all your eggs in one basket."

"Very good," said the teacher.

Next, Mary said, "We are farmers, too. We had twenty eggs waiting to hatch, but when they did we only got ten chicks. The moral of this story is not to count your chickens before they're hatched."

"Very good," said the teacher again, very pleased with the responses so far.

Now, it was Barney's turn to tell his story: "My dad told me this story about my Aunt Karen.... Aunt Karen was a flight engineer in the war and her plane got hit. She had to bail out over enemy territory and all she had was a bottle of whisky, a machine gun, and a machete."

"Go on," said the teacher, intrigued.

"Aunt Karen drank the whisky on the way down to prepare herself; then she landed right in the middle of a hundred enemy soldiers. She killed seventy of them with the machine gun until she ran out of bullets. Then she killed twenty more with the machete till the blade broke. And then she killed the last ten with her bare hands."

"Good heavens," said the horrified teacher. "What did your father say was the moral of that frightening story?"

"Stay away from Aunt Karen when she's been drinking."

AUTHOR UNKNOWN

We ought to think we are one
of the leaves of a tree, and the
tree is all humanity.
We cannot live without the
others, without the tree.

PABLO CASALS

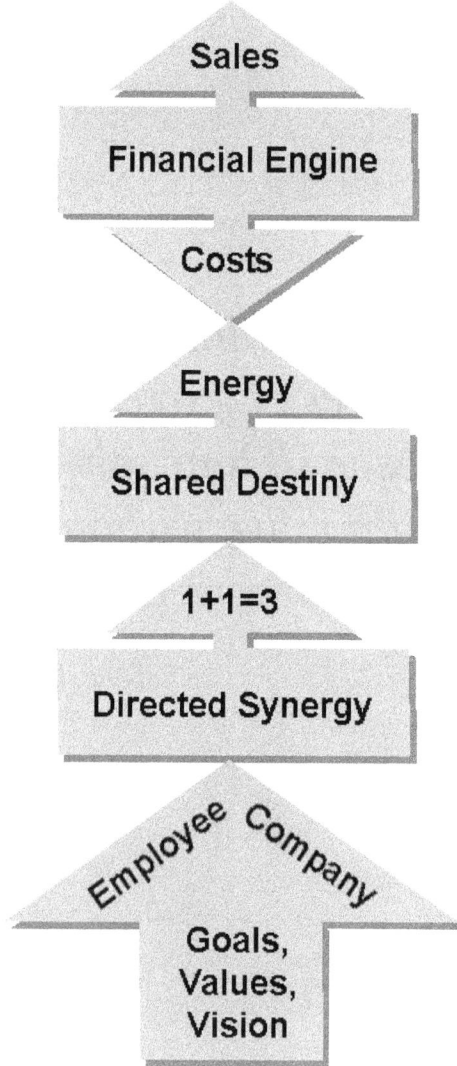

Figure 5. Business Goal-setting Model.

Business Goal Setting

Business goal setting includes all the characteristics of personal goal setting and must be viewed as a vehicle for achieving individual as well as collective success. If executives see themselves achieving personal and family goals through the achievement of a company goal, they willingly take ownership and accountability for the work and steps required for attainment. A good strategic plan needs to include the passion, commitment, focused energy, and alignment of the entire team behind a clearly defined goal.

Setting Goals

1. Do you have a clear set of financial goals?

2. Do you have an overall "WOW" factor goal— the shared destiny goal?

3. Do you have clearly defined business development goals?

4. Do you have executive development goals?

5. Do you have values-based work ethic goals?

1. Do you have a clear set of financial goals?

Financial goals are not just budgets and sales goals, or simple annual arbitrary percentage increases over last year. The key is to always have goals working in two directions: reducing costs and increasing revenues. Financial goals are specific to the larger growth goals (5-10 year vision) with a very specific eye on managing the day-to-day business steps of fulfilling long-term sustainable success.

Daily, weekly, and monthly goals work on labor costs, executive expenditures, staffing costs, controlled growth costs (uncontrolled growth can bring about insurmountable problems), product development, marketing, cost of sales, advertising, etc., all of which are mostly about procuring better deals or finding ways to reduce costs and still maintain ever-increasing value for the dollar spent.

2. Do you have an overall "WOW" Factor goal—the shared destiny goal?

This goal is set for the entire organization. All other goals should line up behind it. It must be compelling, exciting, and understood by everyone. This goal focuses primarily on growth and increasing revenues. Like all change, the attainment of a shared destiny needs to be marketed internally and sold to the team who will then put in the energy to manifest it into reality.

It has to engender passion and must be aligned with the core offering, *core* competencies, and *core* values to make it live, be realistic, yet challenging. As with all marketing promotions, catchy slogans help, but effective daily communication and teamwork are the two ingredients that make it happen.

3. Do you have clearly defined business development goals?

Business development goal setting is a creative, out-of-the-box, beyond the norm process. This is one of the keys to creating great wealth and new opportunities for a company. It is a way to leverage and maximize your core competencies and explore new ways of doing business.

The May 12, 2008 issue of *Fortune Magazine* reports that Larry Page, president of Google, has pushed his people to take risks that have led to hot new applications like gmail and Google Maps. He thinks far outside the walls of his company, ranging from energy to safer cars.

Larry Page is an optimist and has a global view of business, and I encourage you and your team to think in these terms.

Grow your people and they will grow your business!

4. Do you have executive development goals?

This is an area that needs special attention. Your talented individuals need to be challenged and developed. Businesses are only as good as the "right" people, and the right people are hard to find.

An alternative is to train and develop selected individuals. You can keep your ambitious goal-driven managers satisfied by helping them grow in different areas of business development. Give them projects and growth areas to stretch them and keep their need for growth satisfied. You can reinforce your culture and gain a strategic advantage by developing a group of well-groomed and trained executives who are ready and capable for promotion when the need arises. It's a great succession planning strategy.

Some companies are afraid that if they spend money on training their executives, competitors will try to recruit them. That will happen from time to time—it's unavoidable. Good executives will always be sought after—training or not—however, if your culture is strong and a career path has been created and clearly communicated, it reduces the possibility of one of your team accepting offers from head hunters and recruiters. Most progressive leaders take the viewpoint that the cost benefit ratio is beneficial because it attracts the right kind of executive who wants to grow, and moves the business forward by producing great results.

5. Do you have values-based work ethic goals?

Inconsistency in clearly defining and communicating time, energy, and productivity goals creates functional and departmental silos. It breaks down commitment and builds cognitive dissonance, a non-trusting "we/them" atmosphere. Work expectations and respect for personal commitments to families should be embraced and even insisted upon. Working hard, discipline, doing it right the first time, teamwork, and going the extra mile are all great values and work well for businesses—but are not sustainable if the leadership does not appreciate diligent efforts. Success must be recognized and congratulated. Honest and good effort must be appreciated. Everyone needs an energy boost, and positive reinforcement does the trick. Research has shown that a well-paced workforce, with the right recognition, adequate rest, and recovery time is by far a more stable, more productive, and happier workforce.

Goals must be directed toward making a profit, increasing sales, decreasing costs, improving productivity and performance, and should build and take the business to the next level in line with the vision. A strategic plan is incomplete without clearly defined goals and expectations for the entire team.

Amazing achievements materialize when a clear vision, clear values, and purpose are written down in an action plan. The fire and desire to transform individuals and companies from ordinary to extraordinary—from good to great and ultimately to world-class—comes about with the determination, courage, and discipline to materialize the vision into physical reality.

Characteristics of Goal Setting
1. The goal must have a time limit.

Time limits are important because they create a sense of urgency and neutralize the thief-of-time, procrastination. A do-it-now mentality creates the right motivational tension. The right amount of tension directs energy, excitement, and focus, and leads to consistent satisfying results from individuals, teams, and the company.

Timing is everything!

2. The goal must be realistic and challenging.

If you set unrealistic goals, you will de-motivate your team, thus turning tension into demobilizing stress and creating a culture of stagnation (nothing seems to take off). Great care must be taken to set goals that are achievable with the right amount of stretch to create the belief of achievability and the enthusiasm and tension to make it happen. As realistic goals are achieved, platforms of confidence are created and your team will willingly reset continuous incremental sub-goals. As each sub-goal is achieved, confidence grows. I have seen this prudent and patient strategy achieve success over and over. Increasing sales by 2% is completely possible and bearable—and can be accomplished easily, on a regular basis. You achieve extraordinary results by using the power of compounding growth and motivational intelligence. A 2% monthly increase in most businesses is quite acceptable and possible. Two percent compounded is an annual increase of 28%!

3. The goal must be written down in detail.

Written goals take on greater intensity because of the clarity of expectations. Written goals will narrow down focus to relevant issues and activities and become a platform for ongoing communication to redirect and reward efforts and achievements.

4. The goal must be clearly communicated.

Clearly communicating organizational expectations and team expectations cannot be overemphasized. In all the companies I've worked for, the one common area that has consistently created conflict, misunderstanding, dismissal, and lawsuits is the lack of importance placed on proactive communications and clearly detailed expectations.

Jack Welch, in his book *Winning*, talks about the 4E framework he communicated over many years to build the management team at General Electric:

The first E is for Energy. People with energy are communicators, extroverted, and optimistic.

The second E is the ability to Energize others into action.

The third E is for Edge. This is the courage to make tough decisions and face challenges head-on realistically.

The fourth E is for Execute. The ability to get the job done. This means how to put decisions into action and clearly communicate the goal through resistance, chaos, and obstacles.

5. The goal must be aligned to the vision, values, and mission, and measured on a regular basis.

As with the vision and values, acceptability and goal ownership will strengthen the potential for success.

Goal alignment, however, should include a coaching and training session on how individuals can achieve their personal goals through achieving company goals. This is where synergism can take a firm hold. When you show someone how they can fulfill their dreams, you win their hearts and minds instantly. When a leadership team takes the time to establish the key motivational hot buttons of individual employees, it energizes a power source leading to inevitable success. This is what Buckminster Fuller meant when he said: "Real wealth is knowing how to direct energy."

In Summary ...

1. The goal must have a time limit.

2. The goal must be realistic and challenging.

3. The goal must be written down in detail.

4. The goal must be clearly communicated.

5. The goal must be aligned to the vision, values, and mission, and measured on a regular basis.

Once you have set your goals, you have completed the initial work of designing your mission statement. The next important step is to integrate these statements (vision, values, and goals) into one common team mission statement. This is where patience, perseverance, and the belief in teamwork must prevail.

Values and goals are the physical drivers that will move you toward your vision. Once you have a critical mass of ownership, you will discover that you have released an incredible amount of innovative and problem-solving brainpower and ability. Your business will begin to accelerate. Keeping your organization on track during accelerated growth requires a lot of patience, understanding, and skillful knowledge about managing change.

If you don't manage change, change will manage you!

Tickle Me Elmo

The legend has is it that a new employee was hired at the Tickle Me Elmo factory and she duly reported for her first day's induction training, prior to being allocated a job on the production line. At 08:45 the next day, the personnel manager received a visit from an excited assembly line foreman who was not pleased about the performance of the new recruit. The foreman explained that she was far too slow, and that she was causing the entire line to back-up, delaying the whole production schedule.

The personnel manager asked to see what was happening, so both men proceeded to the factory floor. On arrival they saw that the line was indeed badly backed-up. There were hundreds of Tickle Me Elmos strewn all over the factory floor, and they were still piling up. Almost buried in a mountain of toys sat the new employee earnestly focused on her work. She had a roll of red plush fabric and a bag of marbles.

The two men watched amazed as she cut a little piece of fabric, wrapped it around a pair of marbles, and carefully began sewing the little package between Elmo's legs. The personnel manager began to laugh, and it was some while before he could compose himself. He approached the trainee. "I'm sorry," he said to her, not able to disguise his amusement, "but I think you misunderstood the instructions I gave you yesterday.... Your job is to give Elmo two test tickles."

Clearly communicate expectations!

AUTHOR UNKNOWN

90

Vision, Values, Goals, and Mission Statement Examples

Cosmetic Company
Vision:

We see ourselves building an internationally successful business by bringing out the best in everyone and everything we touch. By the best, we mean manufacture the best products, hire the best people, and implement the best ideas. These three pillars form our company and by staying true to them we will build success for our employees, customers, partners, and shareholders.

Values:

We are dedicated to practicing our core values: quality, service, integrity, diversity, and teamwork.

We know we are practicing the values of *quality* when we:

- practice continuous improvement;

- have measurable outcomes;

- practice accountability, efficiency, and positive safe work procedures.

We know we are practicing *service* when we:

- go the extra mile for internal and external customers;
- respond positively to requests from internal and external customers;
- build our brand by meeting deadlines and practicing the highest quality in everything we do.

We know we are practicing *integrity* when we:

- do the right thing at all times;
- encourage trust by being responsible, accountable, and competent;
- conducting ourselves in a trustworthy manner.

We know we are practicing *diversity* when we:

- treat everyone with respect;
- value differences and appreciate the values and beliefs of others;
- create an atmosphere of inclusion.

We know we are practicing *teamwork* when we:

- recognize that teamwork is less "me" and more "we";

- communicate effectively, listen actively, and willingly share information across functions and departments;

- work together to improve everyday work issues that move all of us forward.

Goals:

Our goal is to build a $1 billion international business in alignment with our vision and our values. We will achieve this by expanding our distribution network into every state in the U.S. by 2012. Simultaneously, we will form strategic alliances and partners in Europe, Australia, South Africa, and the Far East that are aligned with our vision, values, and goals.

Mission Statement:

Our mission is to create success for employees, customers, and shareholders by bringing out the best in everyone we touch. By the best we mean, the best products, the best people, and the best ideas.

Urban Development Company
Vision:

Our vision is to be the preferred provider of extraordinary life-enhancing home solutions.

Values:

We will operate as an entrepreneurial organization by:

- exceeding customer's expectations and rewarding the accomplishments of others;

- focusing on continuous improvement;

- thinking and acting with a sense of urgency;

- getting employees to participate in the decision-making process.

We will treat everyone with respect by:

- treating all employees with equal dignity and in a manner that we would want to be treated;

- focusing on the strengths of others;

- appreciating, recognizing, and rewarding the accomplishments of others;

- appreciating, recognizing, and rewarding the loyalty of others;

- controlling negative emotions.

We will act with integrity by:

- consistently meeting commitments and keeping agreements–our word is our bond;

- being open, honest, and direct in a positive manner;

- being non-defensive when responding to others;

- accepting responsibility and accountability for all of our actions.

We will always be a benefit to our community by:

- supporting free enterprise;

- supporting home ownership for all;

- meeting our responsibility to our family and community;

- being good citizens.

Goals:

- we will operate as an entrepreneurial organization;

- we will treat everyone with respect;

- we will act with integrity;

- we will always be a benefit to our community.

Mission Statement:

Our mission is to be an industry leader focused on providing superior homes and service, and earning customer loyalty and outstanding shareholder value.

This will be achieved by developing a professional environment that fosters:

- teamwork with mutual respect;
- commitment;
- integrity;
- innovation; and
- individual trust and responsibility.

Alternative Energy Company (start-up) Vision:

Our vision is to be a leading, well-branded, profitable solar power business with a professional, highly trained, and respected workforce. We see ourselves providing high quality services and products to homeowners, commercial enterprises, and government agencies. We see our solar panels on every rooftop in the nation.

Values:

Our values are:

- profitability through quality, products, and services;

- professionalism in all we do;

- teamwork makes the dream work;

- responsibility in decisions and actions;

- respect for individuals and company;

- continuous improvement;

- communication at all levels;

- trustworthiness, accountability, and execution;

- fun work environment.

Goals:

Our goals are:

- to build a profitable business within 2 years;

- to become one of the largest integrators within the 5 western states in 5 years;

- to support our national goal to be free of our independence on foreign oil;

- to become a fully-fledged, well-respected, and highly profitable green industry company.

Mission Statement:

Our mission is to be a world-class, highly profitable, and well-respected alternative energy company. We believe that our core values form the culture of our business, and our culture will drive and sustain our vision and goals.

Bad planning on your part does not constitute an emergency on my part . . . unless you are a valued customer!

Slogan Examples

Disney: The happiest place on earth.

Ritz Carlton Hotel: We are ladies and gentlemen serving ladies and gentlemen.

Boeing (1950): Become the dominant player in commercial aircraft and bring the world into the jet age.

Sony (1950): Become the company most known for changing the worldwide poor quality image of Japanese products.

IBM: Our goal is simply stated. We want to be the best service organization in the world.

Ford Motor Company (early 1890): Ford will democratize the automobile.

Wal-Mart: To give ordinary folk the chance to buy the same things as rich people. (1990) Become a $125 billion company by the year 2000.

Nike: Just do it! No finish line.

Mary Kay Cosmetics: To give unlimited opportunity to women.

3M: To solve unsolved problems innovatively.

Merck: To preserve and improve human life.

Lennar: Quality, Value, and Integrity.

Figure 6. Step 2.

Step Two

SWOT Analysis

A SWOT analysis is a powerful grounding strategic planning tool, used to effectively assess and evaluate an organization's:

- Strengths
- Weaknesses
- Opportunities
- Threats

Strengths and weaknesses focus on the organization's internal environments and assist the strategic planning process by helping maximize strengths and set goals to overcome or rectify weaknesses. Opportunities and threats mainly focus on the external environment and will help your organization discover new areas of opportunity and plan for and avoid looming and impending dangers.

How to Use a SWOT Analysis

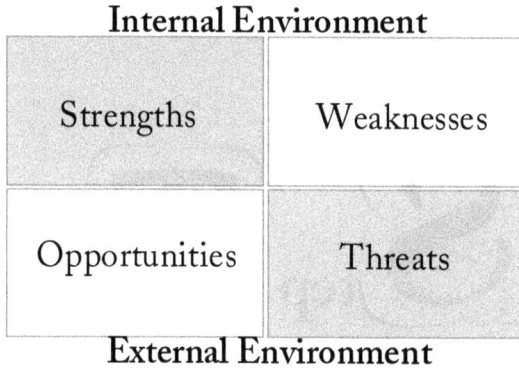

Internal Environment

Strengths	Weaknesses
Opportunities	Threats

External Environment

SWOT analysis should be facilitated by a professional consultant. The use of an outside expert and change agent maintains objectivity and is of great value in creating balance, allowing all voices to contribute.

SWOT analysis should be conducted in a retreat environment and is more effective as a group dynamic interactive project—sharing, investigating, and debating facts, viewpoints, and opinions. This is the power of SWOT: It will bring you closer to reality, and reality is of key importance. Reality and facing the facts—rather than supposition—are the overriding mindsets that should prevail while conducting a SWOT analysis.

SWOT Analysis Questions

What are our Strengths?

- What are our company's general strengths?

- What are our core competencies?

- What are our unique core offerings?

- What are we great at doing—our *piéce-de-resistance*—outstanding accomplishments?

- What can we do better than our competitors?

- What drives our financial engine?

- What is our "WOW" factor—what's unique, special, different, and world-class about our product, service, or people—our *je ne sais quoi?*

- What drives and motivates our team?

- What is our greatest passion?

What are our Weaknesses?

- What do we need to improve to build our business?

- What are customers seeing as our weaknesses (e.g., consistent complaints)?

- What is the weakest link in the business—is it customer service, teamwork, leadership, marketing, staff commitment, staff selection, etc.?

- What are the gaps in our systems and processes that create organizational rework, confusion, or loss of customers? (Note: SWOT analysis may lead to a specific gap analysis process. The author has designed specific flow chart analysis projects to pinpoint gaps in work flow and systems).

What are our Opportunities?

- What are the changes in the industry from which we might benefit?

- What horizontal and vertical opportunities exist for our business?

- Into what new business areas, products, or international markets can we expand?

- What can we do ahead of the competition that will create competitive advantage?

- What are our competitors *not doing* that will allow us to differentiate ourselves?

What are our Threats?

- What economic forecasts or trends can alter the success of our business?

- What new competitors are entering the marketplace?

- What government, political, or regulatory process could interfere with our success?

- What key executives or staff members may we lose?

- What new industries/technology may affect our longevity?

- Are we confident with reinventing, change, and new brand development?

- Have we made *change* a source of strength rather than a source of stress?

The SWOT analysis should be conducted at divisional, departmental, team, and personal levels. It is the second step in your strategic planning process.

The third step in the strategic planning process lays out all the execution essentials necessary to begin the process of manifesting a strategic plan into reality, which is followed by the fourth and final step: "What gets measured gets done."

SWOT Analysis Examples

Home Building Company

$\mathcal{S}$trengths	$\mathcal{W}$eaknesses
• Senior management commitment. • Powerful lead people. • Extensive urban experience. • Focused on a high demand product in a high demand marketplace. • Cutting edge design and product. • Clarity of organizational systems and processes. • Well structured financially.	• Recently formed team. • A relatively narrow exposure of the potential for urban products. • A lack of diversity of products. • Senior housing; "For Rent" apartments; student housing; workforce housing; and commercial/retail development. • Internal communications.
$\mathcal{O}$pportunities	$\mathcal{T}$hreats
• An opportunity to think in financially creative ways. • To partner with developers and private financiers. • Get into rental apartment, commercial developments; and student housing; • General contractor opportunities. • Creating a sense of place, not just a high-density project. • Local market dominance gaps. • Form public and private partnerships. • Entitle and sell land/GC entitled projects.	• Construction costs. • Housing market slowdown. • Media. • Building constraints. • Density issues. • Housing affordability. • Length of entitlement and construction process. • Financing. • Construction defect litigation. • Force majeure.

Shoe Manufacturer and Distributor

$\mathcal{S}$trengths	$\mathcal{W}$eaknesses
• Contracts with about 300 stores. • Has offices in 15 countries, and manages factories in China, Indonesia, and Taiwan. • Employs more than 10,000 people worldwide. • Has a strong marketing strategy and brand that is well recognized by athletes and sportsmen worldwide. • Operates a chain of retail stores. • Is growing through acquisitions and re-branding. • Is positioned to expand the brand into other products. • Uses special exclusive materials to reduce the weight of shoes.	• A lack of transparency regarding information concerning our partnering companies. • Contract manufacturers in China, Vietnam, Mexico, and Indonesia. • Violated overtime laws and minimum wage rates. • Provide poor working conditions and tend to exploit cheap workforces overseas in free trade zones. • Contract overseas companies that apply non-transparent and inadequate labor regulations –involving child labor.
$\mathcal{O}$pportunities	$\mathcal{T}$hreats
• We are able to produce sportswear products from manufacturing waste. • We support eco-friendly projects aimed at further recycling. • Greater emphasis on our global marketing and expansion strategy through the promotion of our brand and core values.	• Textile industry adversely affects the environment and therefore the company is permanently under scrutiny to maintain its eco-friendly reputation. • The current economy may lead to layoffs in a number of our subsidiaries resulting in quality, service, and delivery problems. • Environmental groups who create negative publicity due to our overseas manufacturers who have poor working conditions.

Fast Food Company

$\mathcal{S}$trengths

• Good innovation and product development. We continually innovate to retain our customers.

• Our brand offers consumers choice, reasonable value, and great service.

• Large investments have gone into supporting our franchise network –80% of our stores are franchises.

• Loyal and well-trained staff and strong management team.

$\mathcal{W}$eaknesses

• Core products are out of line with the trend towards healthier lifestyles for adults and children. Product line heavily focused towards hot food and burgers.

• Seasonal sales.

• Limited brand awareness in specific markets.

$\mathcal{O}$pportunities

• Joint ventures with retailers (e.g., supermarkets).

• Consolidation of retailers likely, so better location availability for franchisees.

• Development of healthy menus.

• Strengthen our value proposition and broaden our product menu to encourage customers to visit more regularly.

• Greater focus on corporate social responsibility.

• International expansion into emerging markets in Europe, China, India, and South Africa.

$\mathcal{T}$hreats

• Government and consumer groups encouraging balanced meals–5 fruits and vegetables a day.

• Focus by consumers on nutrition and healthier lifestyles.

• Competitive pressures on the high street as competitors are offering value and greater product ranges and healthier lifestyle products.

• Recession may affect retail sales–as household budgets tighten–reducing spending and the number of visitors.

• Environmental and food pressure groups.

SWOT Analysis Worksheet

$\mathcal{S}$trengths	$\mathcal{W}$eaknesses

$\mathcal{O}$pportunities	$\mathcal{T}$hreats

The Chicken Tests

Engineers at a major aerospace company were instructed to test the effects of bird-strikes on the windshields of airliners and military jets. To simulate the effect of a bird colliding with an aircraft traveling at high speed, the test engineers built a powerful gun with which they fired dead chickens at the windshields. The simulations using the gun and the dead chickens worked extremely effectively, happily proving the strength of the windshields. The success of the tests resulted in several articles about the project in the testing industry press.

It so happened that another test laboratory in a different part of the world was involved in assessing bird-strikes—in this case on the windshields and drivers' cabs of new, very high-speed trains. The train test engineers had read about the pioneering test developed by the aerospace team, and so they approached them to ask for specifications of the gun and the testing methods. The aerospace engineers duly gave them details, and the train engineers set about building their own simulation.

The simulated bird-strike tests on the train windshields and cabs produced shocking results. The supposed state-of-the-art shatterproof, high-speed train windshields offered little resistance to the high-speed chickens; in fact, every single windshield submitted for testing was smashed to pieces, along with a number of train cabs and much of the test booth itself.

The horrified train engineers were concerned that the new high-speed trains required a safety technology that was beyond their experience, so they contacted the aerospace team for advice and suggestions, sending them an extensive report of the tests and failures.

The brief reply came back from the aero-engineers: "You need to defrost the chickens."

AUTHOR UNKNOWN

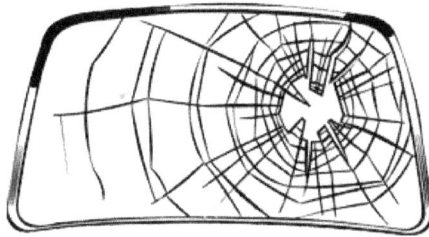

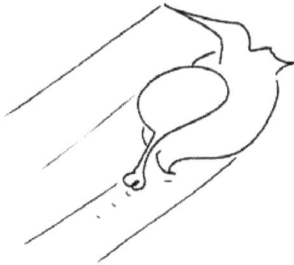

Asking the right questions, leads to the right solutions!

Figure 7. Step 3.

$\mathcal{S}$tep $\mathcal{T}$hree

Execution Essentials

A History of Organizational Structures

Control and Command

Control and Command structures are the oldest structures on Earth and were originally used by armies to organize and mobilize troops and logistics. These structures are top-down and designed to control decisions, and maintain and concentrate power at the top. As organizational structures, they were successful in their time. They were employed to build the Great Wall of China, the Pyramids, the Parthenon, and the Roman Empire; and history is full of examples where power was concentrated at the top. During the industrial revolution, these structures prevailed and were embraced by industrialists. Labor was plentiful and people were prepared to work at a low wage. As we study business history, we notice many great things were achieved through these structures. They worked well in an age where the few ruled and the many were "beholden" to them.

As the industrial revolution progressed and factories became more mechanized and geographically spread out, more people needed to be educated to fill the needs of progress. The advocates of control and command were naturally uneasy with letting go, and wanted to maintain power. However, times were changing rapidly and to remain competitive, power needed to flow downward.

> Business birth is very intoxicating and power is hard to give up.

Multinational markets forced thinking to change and a flatter structure was born. To maintain control, the culture and systems became more regulated with stringent rules and harsher consequences, making workplaces competitive and fearful. A focus on short-term results and a strict adherence to quarterly budgetary compliance became the new way of maintaining power and a determining factor as to whether you kept your job or not. Internal competitiveness became the new method of control.

The Competitive Structure

Abraham Maslow said: "When the only tool you have is a hammer, everything looks like a nail." Internal competition dissipates energy and the focus is largely on each other rather than the organization's overall goal. It creates an uneasy, insecure environment that breeds fear, hostility, and a high degree of back-stabbing. At the same time, fear creates a sense of urgency and things get done quickly, mostly to ensure job security. Unfortunately, the threat of being fired affects the quality of work and costs run much higher. Loyalty to the customer takes on a less important role, real loyalty is virtually nonexistent, and litigation costs escalate. Competitive structures do have redeeming qualities. If you are talented and you are mentally tough, you can move up through the organization quickly and be rewarded quite handsomely. But, as many executives have discovered, it can end rather quickly.

Competitive structures, like traditional structures, demand that the employee worship the boss and the data. This sets the standards: Fear the boss! Fear the data! The boss gets all the attention and employees compete with each other to gain recognition. They jockey for office positioning and company function positioning. I have seen the emotional impact of this style on junior employees. Their days are either up or down depending on a simple acknowledgment from the boss. Needless to say, this is a highly political environment and if you are a good game player, you do well.

The underlying assumption made by the proponents of both control and command, and competitive structures, is that at some level people are not smart enough, are inherently lazy, dislike work and, therefore, need to be supervised with a high level of control (Theory X—McGregor). During the industrial revolution, that worked well because society was more conformist and citizens and families were controlled through patriarchal, religious, political, and bureaucratic rules; regulations; and norms. But as history has shown us, this structure is now obsolete.

History is fraught with revolutions: the French Revolution, the Russian Revolution, the Declaration of Independence, the Berlin Wall, apartheid, and more recently, capital socialism in China. Business in the free world has had its revolts against dictatorial leadership in whatever form or disguise it might present itself. The trade union movements were given birth as a voice against unfair labor practices. Ironically, many unions now employ command and control, and competitive structures to control their organizations.

The interesting change that has come about in the last fifteen years—but even more so recently—is the recognition that these structures are as outdated as the technology of the past and that the new worker is demanding a new workplace: a different way of working together. There is a social revolution happening—a critical mass of younger employees are looking for change, a change from the old way of doing things to new ways to belong and contribute. The majority of X, Net, and Millennial generations are wanting a greater say in the things that affect them. They want meaningful work that has a sense of purpose. They don't want and will not tolerate the old top-down styles of management. They simply will not work for them. They are comfortable with change, want change, and want to be a part of creating the future. They are excited by technology, cooperation, and the loyalty of relationships, and they want leaders they can learn from and admire.

The recent landslide elections in the U.S. clearly demonstrate this point. Change is wanted and comes in the form of collaborative effort, high-performance teamwork with a focus on a value-driven, shared destiny. The Internet and all its communication speed, and the sharing of ideas is a huge synergistic structure that connects anyone to everyone. E-Bay, Google, and Facebook are the new avenues of business communication and social interaction.

Technology -> Synergy -> Transparency

The Synergistic Structure

Synergistic Structures lead with a clearly defined vision, a clear set of goals, core values, and purpose-driven leaders who believe that value-driven organizations will always be more successful in the long term. For years, I have known that the most successful businesses were all about alignment, integration, and integrity, and that their leaders were the opposite of the hyped-up image of those portrayed by Enron, Worldcom, and all the others involved in the mortgage and banking fiasco. One day I received an advance copy of Jim Collins' *Good to Great* book. As I read his empirical research on Level 5 leaders, my years of coaching experience and knowledge about what made a successful leader were validated. What a great day that was!

> *"We were surprised, shocked really, to discover the type of leadership required for turning a good company into a great one. Compared to high-profile leaders with big personalities who make headlines and become celebrities, the good-to-great leaders seem to have come from Mars. Self-effacing, quiet, reserved, even shy – these leaders are a paradoxical blend of personal humility and professional will. They are more like Lincoln and Socrates than Patton or Caesar."*
> JIM COLLINS, GOOD TO GREAT, 2001

In all the successful companies I have worked with, leadership is encouraged at all levels of the organization, and empowerment is seen as a strategic advantage, rather than a loss of power. Synergistic Structures attract talented individuals who see that the leadership culture and structure allows them the opportunity to grow and develop. They are secure within themselves and are willing to work with and share knowledge with other secure individuals. Synergistic Structures and the leaders who implement them are passionate about their work and see work as fun, exhilarating, and "can't-wait-to-get-started." Synergistic leaders are acutely aware that real wealth is knowing how to direct energy. Human beings are best when they are relaxed and feel a sense of belonging, regardless of gender, race, age, size, or religious beliefs. With a Synergistic Structure and culture, change becomes a source of strength rather than a source of stress. You are part of a high-performance team. High-performance teamwork is demanding and difficult, and not that easy to accomplish. Each person must be trusted to perform in a responsible, reliable, and responsive way. It's a self-policing system with no place to hide. Everybody is trusted to do their best—if they don't, *the team* will let them go. The most profitable companies in a variety of industries employ Synergistic Structures of one kind or another: Southwest Airlines, Nordstroms, Google, Starbucks, E-Bay, and Facebook to name just a few.

Alignment of Systems and Processes to Strategy, Culture, People, and Leadership

Organizational systems are critical to success. You can have extremely talented individuals and teams, but if your systems are poor, you will not achieve the success you envisioned. You can have really good systems and average people, and you will only be averagely successful. If you have well-thought-out systems and you back them up with a strong culture and talented individuals working in teams, you have a winning formula that will make you extremely successful.

When physical, mental, and emotional energy are in sync, supported by a great system and aligned toward a shared destiny, success is a given.

List of general systems:

- information;
- performance;
- compensation;
- hiring;
- training and development;
- reporting;
- administrative;
- accounting;
- manufacturing;

- customer care;

- career pathing;

- cultural and values maintenance process;

- human resources;

- budgetary; and

- staff exit process.

All these systems must be aligned with the mission and fused with the core values and culture. When this happens 1+1=3 . . . or more!

How to Write a Strategic Plan

Writing out a detailed Synergy Strategic Plan is the responsibility of the senior executive team and is a prerequisite to success. In essence, you are writing out the Constitution for your business and what, where, when, why, who, and how you want it to happen.

This is your blueprint for success and your platform for decision-making, and therefore requires thought, leadership, and full ownership to guide it through to victory.

This is a CEO, COO, CFO hands-on process and requires an executive team commitment. Synergy Strategic Planning can be likened to orchestrating and writing a symphony of strategic and operational excellence. It begins with creative composition and vision followed by manifesting it into writing, many times rewriting it until it's so clear that all that's required are the action steps for its fulfillment.

A good symphony of operational excellence includes key managers and divisional heads from different operating units to help orchestrate, conduct, and align different sections of the business to ensure that everyone is playing from the same sheet of music. Involving and empowering operational leaders and influencers to think strategically stands the greatest chance of ownership to a shared destiny, and builds the greatest possible synergy of people, systems, and processes at all levels of the organization.

Mission Statement

Write out a summarized internal mission statement. Make the mission statement a motivational connector. Make it exciting and energizing. The mission construction is covered in detail in Step One of this book—use it as your guide. Include your company's overall core values and talk through the principles, standards, and non-negotiable areas that will need to be practiced by the majority of your team. It is important to reach an overall agreement and commitment to individual and team expectations to avoid the conflicts that can arise from not knowing clearly what's required.

Passion infused into the musical notes always exhilarates the audience!

Clearly Define Goals

It is imperative to establish specific execution goals if you want to materialize the vision. Your team needs to have clear direction and focus to deliver effectively. People follow leaders that are confident and sure about the journey ahead.

It is also important to create clearly-defined goals for each team member. Make sure the company goals you want to achieve will assist them in getting what they want in their lives. Once you find out what they want (their hot buttons), it is easier to help them set and achieve their goals while also achieving company goals. A good plan connects personal and company goals and effectively directs energy. If team members want to buy a new house or give their kids a great education, and you can help them see that all of those things are attainable, then personal motivation and commitment will follow as surely as day follows night.

The "WOW" Factor! Goal: This is a stretch goal. It is a compelling goal designed to ignite, and stir up team passions and excitement. "WOW, if we could make this happen . . ." must be on everyone's lips. A passionate leadership focus and commitment from your strongest and most committed team players will energize the rest of the team, creating a critical mass of ownership, and *that* will make it happen. The mission, values, and goals part of your strategic plan should be treated as an internal marketing message—

a message that you should drive and promote, advertise, and sell with the same vigor used to launch a new product.

Complete a SWOT Analysis

A SWOT analysis will assist your team avoid the pitfalls often overlooked in the planning process. A SWOT analysis begins the process of realistically measuring Strengths, Weaknesses, Opportunities, and Threats; balances collective viewpoints; and opens up many areas of the business to scrutiny. Realistically ask the question: "Have we considered all internal and external factors in our SWOT analysis?"

SWOT analysis requires F.A.D.—Fanatical Attention to Detail. Clear-headed, precise thinking will assist the smooth execution of your plan. Ask your team "What if?" questions and scan all high- and low-road possibilities. Project both positive and negative outcomes by going through the possibilities: "What would the impact be on your business and what would you do?" "What would the contingency plan look like if certain things didn't happen?" and so on. This critical and evaluative approach builds a sense of certainty, reduces the stress impact of market changes, and brings a sense of assurance that success is a well-thought-out and planned set of progressive steps toward the realization of a worthy shared destiny. Once you have completed the SWOT analysis, reassess your mission and goals before writing up your execution strategy.

A Leadership Commitment

Once again, leadership commitment is required to carry a strategic plan through to success. This means making a commitment to going the extra mile. It means a commitment to attending training meetings and being engaged on a daily basis with the mission. It means that the vision, values, and goals become the number one operational, driving force and decision-making platform in the business.

Leaders vs. Managers: There is confusion between management and leadership. You can effectively manage systems, processes, schedules, cash flow, and capital, but you can't be as effective managing people as you can if you learn to lead them. People are more effective and produce better results when they are led. Leadership is more difficult because it requires an understanding of human behavior. As a manager, it's much easier to tell people what to do and if they don't do it, you fire them. Easy! But it's different being a leader.

As a leader, you must lead by example; you must show the way. You have to coach, teach, and build a high-performance team. Leading means you are responsible for the success of those you are leading. You can't exclude yourself and lay blame at the feet of your team. The buck stops with *you*. This is not so easy; but it is highly effective in increasing productivity and performance. You just won't get the performance you are looking for using control and command management methods.

Good leadership produces a willing participation, so attrition reduces dramatically, costs come down, and people don't shoot each other!

Clearly Define Expectations

In the physical execution of the plan, it is important to determine a clear reporting structure, goals, time limits, and boundaries. Team members are more motivated when they know who's in charge and what is expected of them. State what you want directly: "This is what I expect from you." Be clear and precise, and then ask, "What do you expect from me and this project?" This kind of "expectation meeting" fosters healthy conversation and builds relationship trust.

To avoid misunderstanding and ambiguity, make sure that your communications are very clear and precise, and that everybody knows exactly what needs to be done. ("What you expect is what you get.") Good strategists demand high expectations and performance from team members. High expectations will always increase the likelihood of high performance. The right amount of tension—not stress—directed toward a goal increases human performance dramatically.

In 1940, President Franklin D. Roosevelt said that to win the war the U.S. needed 50,000 planes a year. He expected America to rise up to the expectation, and they did. John F. Kennedy announced that we would put a man on the moon within the decade. He expected that this breathtaking goal would fire up the national pride, and it did. At first, these goals were considered too high. Yet, at the same time, they were clear, exciting, and breathtaking. America achieved both of these goals in grand fashion and undoubtedly their attainment was hastened by the dramatic Presidential announcements and expectations.

Visionaries need those that naturally practice F.A.D. to make the dream become a reality!

Organizational Detail

The successful achievement of objectives and goals can be directly traced back to the quality of the organization and planning. Time management, time-lines, scheduling, and reporting structure are essential. Successful achievement can be directly traced back to the leadership groups' insight and ability to match talent to function and function to team configuration. Match skills with specific jobs and then form teams made up of personalities that compliment each other.

As mentioned earlier, an important skill is fanatical attention to detail. It always pays off. Checklists, specific methods, and follow-through are of paramount importance. F.A.D. works extremely well in the franchise, hospitality, health, and entertainment industries and, of course, in aerospace where there is no room for error at all. Doing it right the first time and zero defects are achieved because of the attention given to the importance of organizational detail prior to and during the execution of the goal.

Whether the project or strategic plan is company-wide or requires involving other members in different departments, you will need to set up Synergy Team Power Meetings. These meetings are focused on setting up cross-functional goals to assist in the execution of the plan at an operational level. Firm follow-up reporting and progress dates are essential—"What Gets Measured Gets Done." Teach your teams to be disciplined and respectful of reporting dates and agreements. That means that you should be careful to set realistic goals that challenge your team while building confidence at the same time.

Measuring the right things at the right time separates leaders from managers!

Scope of the Goal

Clearly understand the scope of the goal, its size, and determine—with your feet planted solidly on the ground—all the functional steps and resources required to achieve success. The following tools and guidelines will assist you in thinking through your plan.

Ambiguity results in costly overruns!

Project Lifeline

Flow charts are clearly defined charts that map out the steps of the process so that they can be easily understood and communicated to the implementation team. The benefit of a project flow chart is that the entire team is clear about their role in the project. In the larger context, it helps each manager, divisional head, and supervisor evaluate and analyze their particular role and how it links into the overall larger change program.

Using flow charts at the beginning of a change program will enable you to reduce margins of error, while also allowing your team to easily and quickly track the problems by examining if all the steps were taken (or included). This is a great strategic tool that will help you with root-cause analysis and avoid treating symptomatic problems rather than causes.

From a team spirit standpoint, flow charts allow team members to focus on solutions and not on each other. Measurement is a critical aspect of managing a strategic plan. Clearly defined goals, clear expectations, clear job descriptions, and flow charts are the tools that will empower talented individuals to succeed more consistently and with greater speed.

> Flow charts enhance interdepartmental and functional synergies.

Finances

Have budgets been set? Are they realistic? Was the financial team included in the mission creation?

Location

Where and how will teams meet? Have all locations and physical aspects of the plan been considered? Is it possible to cost-effectively use technology to conduct meetings?

Policies

Did you make sure that the strategic plan is aligned with corporate policies? Review policies and procedures manuals or consult with H.R. before you begin.

Strategic Alliances

In today's ever-changing world, strategic partner-ships and alliances are critical; consider how outside partners, consultants, and vendors will play a role in helping the plan succeed.

Technology

Are you currently up to date? How will technology help in cost reduction?

Return on Investment

Do you have clear financial projections and performa income statements?

Does each project focus on the profitability of the business?

How does the ROI energize the financial engine?

The goal of every business is to focus on creating a profitable return on the investment of time, money, and other resources employed.

Responsibility

Clearly define areas of responsibility and allow your teams to talk through their areas of responsibility so they're better able to understand how each team member links in and connects to the process.

Accountability

The great benefit of organizational detail, good planning, and teamwork is that accountability improves and honest reporting is more accepted and less threatening. Teams hold each other accountable and the peer group pressure creates a greater sense of urgency.

Timing

Is the timing realistic? Do the team members have the time to make the project a success?

Eliminate Excuses

Listen to valid reasons—don't accept excuses—and an outstanding thing will happen: Your team will become more self-managing. As each team member becomes tuned into reality, they become more responsible for their actions.

We've all made excuses in our lives (e.g., it was the traffic or the dentist, my wife, my dad, my uncle, my aunt, I didn't have enough information, and so on). Competence is the first pillar of real teamwork. Each team member must be really good at what they do. The second pillar is honesty. If team members are dishonest and make excuses, the team cannot ever trust them completely about anything. When you eliminate excuses and fear, you eliminate interpersonal friction and build a sense of belonging and zones of inspiration.

Right Project Attitude

Abraham Lincoln wisely said: "Folks are just about as happy as they make their minds up to be." When I look at people in my seminars and workshops, I search for those who have made up their minds to be happy; I search for the fire in their eyes. Is there an outer reflection of an inner curiosity? I see many willing, "I'm-ready-to-strategize" eyes but, sadly, I see many defensive, cold, and "keep-your-distance" eyes. Almost always, I'm-ready-eyes contribute *more*, learn *more*, have *more* fun, and communicate *more* effectively.

But then, the magic happens: Slowly, but surely, the keep-your-distance eyes soften, become livelier, and start flickering with curiosity. And before too long, they have shifted their thinking—and once again I'm stunned by the power of positive energy. It is wild fire contagious!

Reward Good Performance

Make individual performance within the team important—but don't make the mistake of putting people up against each other. Make the team the heroes of success and reward the performance and the behaviors that you want repeated. When a particular team does well, bring that whole team in front of the other team members and congratulate them. Congratulate them for their great teamwork, spirit, dedication, and their commitment to the plan.

When you reward your team with positive reinforcement, they celebrate their success together, and repeating good performance becomes easier. Build into your plan specific rewards to motivate change. We all want recognition, to know that we're doing a good job, and to know that we are working with competent people. Competence and trusting relationships build synergistic teamwork, which speeds up productivity and performance.

Synergizing

Team configuration: Who will make up the team? Do you have a good spread? Are the members compatible? Are they secure enough to cooperate and collaborate effectively?

Many people perceive going to work as something they "have to" do, and whenever you have to do anything the energy input is lower and less contagious. Just like high-performance business teams, professional sports teams "want to" play and come in every day because it is perceived as fun, not work; and they willingly want to do so as often as possible. This energy is highly contagious, resulting in extraordinary performance. The key is to change the perception of work from a have-to to a want-to approach, which is achieved through a well-structured strategic plan that includes leadership commitment, high-performance teamwork, a clearly defined vision, a set of core values that reinforces the culture and "WOW" factor goals that are measurable, exciting, and achievable.

As the team grows and develops, creativity becomes the by-product. Creative thinking is something team members rediscover as they learn to trust one another. We are born with creativity, but societal pressures force us to focus on logic and conformity. Unleashing creativity and brainpower is the function and duty of a great strategist. A teacher has never created an ounce of intelligence. Teachers can only condition and train the intellect that already exists.

Your job is to release the brainpower through synergy!

Driving

As you begin to "drive" your strategic plan, you'll find that people will become motivated and excited. As with life, you will hit roadblocks and need to take detours. Dealing with roadblocks proactively—in the right frame of mind—is important. Welcome problems: See them as challenges that allow you and your team to learn new ways to achieve success. When you are leading a project, you are really selling the vision, teamwork, and trust in you and your ability to drive the project until you achieve success. This is what makes the journey stimulating and worthwhile!

Implement Continuous Improvement

The Japanese principle of Kaizen means continuously improving systems, processes, quality, and performance in every way, every day. It is making small, continuous improvements in many different things. It's easy to understand if you remember the movie *What About Bob*. Bob was an extremely neurotic patient whose psychiatrist told him that he could conquer his panic attacks by taking one baby step at a time. He tried it and it worked. In this lighthearted movie, a powerful business principle is revealed. Continuous improvement (Kaizen) is about using "baby steps" to cause, over time, vast improvements. Once you get your entire team working on continuously improving their jobs, within a year your entire organization will have reinvented itself. The strategic goals will be achieved.

Priorities: The Secret Six

A management consultant was asked by a corporation president to help him improve the performance of his top 100 executives. Without a moment's hesitation, the consultant said, "Put them onto a things-to-do-today list and let them try to accomplish the six most important things that have to be done today."

Some months later, the president met with the consultant again and said, "You never sent me a bill for the last consultation."

"If it solved the problem, drop a check in the mail in direct proportion of its value to you."

Three weeks later, the consultant received a check for $10,000.

Fully aware that it's a matter of priority and focus, the consultant knew his advice would work, since he had given it to other clients—and it worked every time.

If you do the six most important things in your life every day, you'll accomplish 1,440 in-the-moment, life-changing experiences per year. Now, that's a simple, powerful, and highly effective formula for success!

Materializing

Once you begin to materialize success, watch out for complacency. The idea that somehow achieving the goal means you have arrived—and so you don't have to make the same effort—is very common, and your greatest enemy. Success can be the enemy of progress. Make sure that you set your next goal before you achieve your current goal, and make sure that you stretch yourself and keep the team excited.

Internal Marketing

Successful strategic planning requires that all members understand their individual functions, what is expected of them, how they will be held accountable, and the goals of the company. A conversation of "what-success-looks-like" is paramount, and an explanation of how management intends to achieve success helps people connect to what they need to do. The more internal marketing and communication, the better. Successful internal execution projects need to be sold in the same way as external marketing projects, such as launching a new product. Clear communications, clear benefits, an outstanding presentation, and enthusiastic demonstrable ownership will win over the most ardent cynics, and lubricate the most difficult plan and make it successful.

The Rollout

Rolling out the internal marketing process is the responsibility of the senior executive and management team.

The Mission Statement Presentation: It is the responsibility of leadership to win the hearts and minds of the entire team. Leadership is a selling process. You must sell the mission, get buy-in on the vision and core values, and commitment to the "WOW" factor goals.

The SWOT Analysis: All members of the management team and key personnel need to be clear on company strengths, weaknesses, opportunities, and threats.

The Strategic Planning Steps must be communicated and made clear to senior management, project team leaders, and all members of the team. The test of success is asking a staff member these two simple questions: "What's our mission, and what are you doing each day to make it happen?"

The Execution is the responsibility of the project managers, department managers, project teams, and team members, supported by a serious commitment from the CEO and senior management team. Ensure that there is a clearly defined reporting structure, along with structured follow-through and Synergy Team Power Meetings to lubricate the process. Do not underestimate the importance of meetings and information sharing at an operational level. The progress of the program must be supported by empowerment, ownership, celebration, and recognition.

How to Write a Strategic Plan Checklist

☐ **Mission Statement**: A written mission statement that includes your vision, values, and general goals.

☐ **Clearly Define Goals**: These are your specific written-out goals, in detail.

☐ **Complete a SWOT Analysis**: This analyzes strengths, weaknesses, opportunities, and threats.

☐ **A Leadership Commitment**: Executive commitment makes all the difference.

☐ **Clearly Define Expectations**: For your team to exceed expectations, you need to define them.

☐ **Organizational Detail**: The quality of organization determines success. *Scope of the Goal:* This determines all the functional steps and resources required to achieve success.

☐ **Eliminate Excuses**: Set high standards and keep the team focused.

☐ **Right Project Attitude**: Create positive energy and direct it to the goal.

☐ **Reward Good Performance**: Reinforce the behavior you want repeated.

☐ **Synergizing**: Team configuration.

☐ **Driving:** All change programs must be championed and driven.

☐ **Implement Continuous Improvement:** Constantly examine ways to improve.

☐ **Priorties: The Secret Six:** Work on key result areas.

☐ **Materializing:** Keep on moving the team forward; avoid the complacency that follows success.

☐ **Internal Marketing:** All change needs to be marketed to be successful.

Portrait of a Leader

Jim was a 20-year Navy veteran when he took a job as the head of a food service department. In addition to purchasing supplies and equipment, inventory control, and menu planning, he was responsible for feeding everyone in an organization that operated year-round and around the clock. As an ex-Navy cook and manager, the schedule was familiar to him, but to his employees, it was an entire change of lifestyle. Most of Jim's employees had little or no experience in food service, so he was responsible for their on-the-job training. Fortunately, Jim had always liked the teaching aspect of management, so he enjoyed training; the pleasure he took in his work also made it enjoyable for his workers. He taught them about hygiene, portion control, nutrition, food preparation, baking, and even meat-cutting.

Once the first employees were competent, he set them to teaching the newcomers what they knew. This strategy freed him up from constant training and let his more seasoned workers add training to their repertory of skills. Without talking about it, he taught his employees about teamwork, so that when they received compliments on an especially fine meal, every person on the team had earned it and felt pride in the accomplishment.

When any team finished work early, Jim would teach them to create foods outside the realm of the institutional menu items they usually worked with. The success of the team might be measured in a proofing cabinet filled with croissants, or twelve dozen fresh, hot, nutmeg-scented doughnuts. Team members tested their recipes and shared their success with people who came to eat in the cafeteria.

The hours were long, often starting before five in the morning, and the work was heavy, but by the time the first year was out, people employed in other parts of the organization were asking Jim if he had openings in his department. He soon had a waiting list, and anyone who didn't want to work up to the standards of the team was replaced with someone who was excited to be on it. After awhile, it got more and more difficult to find team members who didn't measure up. And the food just got better and better.

Jim wasn't interested in hearing excuses or complaints, but he took time to hear what employees had to say about the work environment, and when he saw a chance to improve it, he did. Sometimes he butted heads with his boss, but most of the time the head administrator saw that what Jim did was working, so he left him to his own devices.

An old-fashioned manager by training, Jim was kind of tough and sometimes terse, but when he got angry, he kept it to himself until he decided on the best course of action. He spent minimal amounts of time in his office, and most of his time with the team, teaching and coaching. He told people what he expected of them, taught them how to achieve the *goals of the department, and showed them the rewards of doing the job well. When people left the organization, many who had come to his department with no previous experience got fine jobs based on the work they had done with Jim.*

Jim was an impressive leader: respected, human, straightforward, and determined. Under his leadership, budgetary goals were met or exceeded, work was accomplished on time, and employees grew into competent, responsible cooks. In any organization, managers like Jim are pure, unadulterated gold, but maybe Jim's accomplishment is even more impressive because of the special circumstances of his place of employment. His area of responsibility was the food service department of a state detention facility, and all his employees were convicted felons.

2% of the world's population initiate, innovate, create, and make things happen.

14% criticize, help, or condemn them, while thinking they can do it better.

84% don't know what is going on ... unless the 2% or 14% tell them.

Figure 8. Step 4.

Step Four

What Gets Measured Gets Done

Who the hell is running this place?

It was 10pm. I had just arrived in Las Vegas. Normally, it's a five hour drive from Orange County in California to Las Vegas—but not this time! It took seven grueling hours through El-Nino rain and snowstorms. I was tired, hungry, cold, and ready to get into my pre-booked, prepaid room. I self-parked and walked the half marathon to the registration desk. I was greeted by a line of 20-30 similarly red-eyed, tired, and frustrated people who seemed bewildered and confused, and I soon understood why.

This was the first hotel ever, and I've been in a

few, to force their guests to check themselves in on a computer. This is the same self-check-in process used at airports—except there's one big difference: At airports, they give the tired, dazed, and confused an option, you can deal with a carbon-based life form, or the computer—the choice is yours. This was not the case at this hotel, and to pour more fuel on the fire of disgust, the computers did not work.

"You have to swipe the same credit card you booked with" somebody yelled; "I've tried that and it doesn't work!" someone yelled back. We were all gathered around trying to do the work that we already paid this hospitality establishment to do. It was like a bad comedy scene from a B-rated movie. "Who the hell is running this place?" I heard a woman say as she stormed off. I'm sure she went on to find adequate accommodations at an establishment run by real businesspeople.

Finally, a flurry of movement and three check-in people beckon us to step forward.

"NEXT!" Yippee, that's me! After another long shlep, I finally get up into my room—"Ahhh at last! Oh no!!, the room's not made up!!" For a moment, I was stopped in my tracks and knew instantly that there must be a hidden message in all of this. Then suddenly it hit me! The management of this establishment doesn't care about delivering quality service to its guests. It's not a part of their business philosophy. Getting the customer's money in advance and shortsighted cost cutting is

their gig. It's all about greed and not about customer satisfaction or integrity.

If this hotel management group *did* have integrity, they would be focused on the customer's experience. They would be measuring and improving all the service methods, systems, and processes to take care of *me*, their customer, their revenue source. Of course, very few people are loyal to this sort of business and the cost of attracting new customers continuously is extremely high, even in Las Vegas. So, who are the Neanderthals running these types of businesses, anyway? What are they thinking? Why are they being allowed to make such poor fundamentally stupid decisions? Don't they know that without customers they wouldn't have a business? Isn't that Marketing 101? Maybe they are caught up in those corporate data printouts, and they have to serve the executive gods in the tower instead of the customer. All I can tell you is I'm never going back and won't be surprised to hear that this hotel went out of business.

Measure the Right Things

Business measurement is essential to success. Product quality and service standards are maintained, achieved, and improved through measurement. Total quality management, ISO 9000, and many other systems and processes are tools to increase quality, customer satisfaction, and business efficiency. It is well documented that these processes and measurements reduce costs, and increase revenues and customer loyalty.

Measurement tools come in many different formats. To avoid being seen by employees as policing tools and/ or avoid the misperception that a good result on an audit means automatic completion, the use of measurements must be well communicated prior to implementation. As with all human interaction, a clear description, intention, and collective goal must be communicated.

Without measurement, there is no way of knowing whether you made a good decision or the actions you are taking are moving you forward, sideways, or even backwards.

Measure the right things and you will get the right results, and when you feed information back to your teams and reward success—success repeats itself. Say "WOW" to the world and the world will say "WOW" to you! It is the law of cause and effect.

Customer Satisfaction

Measuring customer satisfaction is vital to profitability and growth and should be taken very seriously. Customer loyalty can be directly linked to the increase in revenue, reduction of advertising costs, and cost of sales. There are several ways to successfully measure customer satisfaction:

- in-house rating surveys;

- J.D. Power and Associates;

- Eliant Inc. (building industry); and

- independent survey companies.

Do not make the mistake of assuming your customers are completely satisfied. On more than one occasion, executive teams I've worked with have been shocked by the low ratings from their first outside, independent survey.

Systems and Processes

The implementation of Total Quality, ISO 9000, or Six Sigma programs assists in creating a culture of synergistic measurement. There are a number of tools available in these programs to assist in tightening up the efficiency of a production line, construction process, and any other process used in service-related industries, such as:

- flow charts;

- fishbone diagrams;

- the total quality PDSA cycle;

- Synergy directional audits; and

- continuous improvement.

Human Resources

Attitudinal surveys reveal how employees feel about management support; values; motivation; teamwork and workplace environment, relationships, and attitudes.

The information gathered from these surveys should always be shared with those surveyed and then followed by specific written-down goals to implement the changes.

Management and Leadership

Three sixty surveys (360°) are extremely effective in analyzing, measuring, and developing executive skills, communication effectiveness, leadership ability, decision-making skills, and team cohesiveness.

The key factors for implementing a 360° feedback survey are:

1. Good preparation.

2. Selecting the right questions.

3. Focused on strengths, not weaknesses.

4. Focused on growth, not reprimand.

5. Inclusive of all executives.

6. Focused on goals for improvement.

7. Followed up with coaching sessions.

Performance Reviews

Performance reviews can be extremely destructive or constructive, depending on how the process is handled. There are a myriad of negative connotations in the words "performance review." Perhaps "personnel appraisal" would be a better phrase. The focus of personnel appraisals should be to:

1. help employees take ownership of the areas in need of improvement;

2. build trust through candid and honest leadership coaching;

3. set realistic, measurable goals for growth; and

4. release talent and brainpower.

Financial Measurement

Financial measurement is critical to success. Without cost controls and measures that ensure adequate funds, a business will not survive. In most well-run organizations, financial measurement data is available on a daily, weekly, and monthly basis. Speedy and accurate financial information is of enormous value to the strategic and operating plans of an organization.

Sales Measurements

For many companies, sales projections determine the difference between success and failure. Sales are the lifeblood of any business, and the measurement must be taken very seriously.

Each salesperson should be measured in:

- actual dollar sales volume;
- customer satisfaction;
- teamwork ability;
- leadership potential;
- drive and determination;
- responsibility, reliability, and responsiveness;
- attitude; and
- integrity.

Staff Selection

Quality-talented individuals who have the right attitude will reduce the frequency and necessity of follow-through and measurement. If you employ individuals who are personally driven to do a good job—rather than being told to—the cost of doing business will reduce dramatically.

Redirection audits and measurement are vital follow-through, accountability, and execution tools.

Execution and accountability of performance are major problems in today's business world. Using a tool or a structured program that focuses on moving the organization forward in a constructive, measurable way energizes the climate and provides managers with a platform for redirection and coaching.

The Synergy Directional Audit

The directional audit is a practical, creative, problem-solving, and measurement process.

As a part of the strategic planning process, measurement questions must be authored and used as a guideline in an explorative, interactive, and information-sharing retreat setting. By using a group of dynamic processes and real questions focused on accountability and execution, truth is inevitable; and ownership, replanning, final execution, and goal achievement are enhanced. I have structured and conducted directional audit processes that have resulted in serious realignment, committed ownership, and extraordinary success.

Synergy Directional Audits are performed to ascertain the validity, credibility, and progress of the set goals and objectives.

Synergy Directional Audits are not just about the financial aspects of a business; they also include other areas that increase revenues and reduce costs, such as:

- customer service;

- marketing;

- teamwork;

- sales;

- management;

- leadership;

- core values;

- vision;

- attitudes;

- environment/climate;

- commitment;

- systems and processes;

- finances; and

- strategic planning.

The single constant to success is leadership style and integrity!

In Conclusion

An African Fable

Put five monkeys in a cage. Hang a banana at the top of the cage with a ladder leading up to it. Soon a monkey will start to climb toward the banana. As soon as he is on the ladder, spray him with cold water.

When another monkey tries to climb the ladder, spray him and the rest of the group. After this experience, if one of the monkeys tries to climb the ladder, the group will stop him.

Now remove one monkey and replace him with a new one. The new monkey will see the banana and try to climb the ladder. To his surprise, the group will attack him.

After a few attempts and attacks he gives up trying. Now replace another monkey with a new one. Predictably, the new one is attacked when he attempts to retrieve the banana. The previous new monkey joins in the attack.

Replace a third one, and he will be attacked as well. It is important to know that two of the four monkeys that attacked this last one did so without knowing why.

After replacing all the monkeys that were originally sprayed, no monkey approaches the ladder ... why not? Because the cage behavior patterns have been set.

AUTHOR UNKNOWN

This happens all the time in the workplace. Whenever you hear the words "that's the way it's always been done around here" or "good luck trying to implement the new mission, we tried that before and it didn't work" . . . it's a red flag that conformity rules.

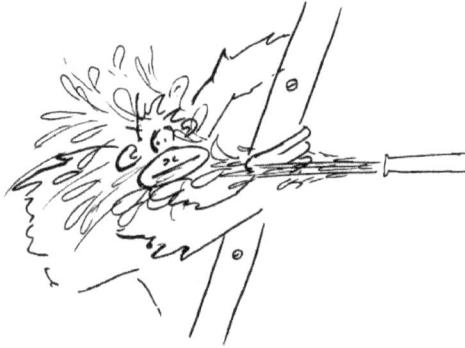

Teach your people to think, and avoid conformity and mediocrity.

Troubleshooting

We've Always "Done-it-that-way" and "We're-already-doing-that"

Whenever you hear these phrases, you will know they are smoke screens for not wanting to change.

Your Actions: Use probing questions to clarify and discover rooted misunderstandings in the culture and obvious gaps in the current process.

Resistance to Change

One of the most serious barriers to change is individual resistance. There are many reasons why people resist change ranging from the insecurity created by the fear of the unknown to the lack of leadership follow-through. Or, maybe flavor-of-the-month stop-start programs have been tried that have left operational managers jaded, saying: "Why should we change? It won't make any difference." Lastly, change sends mixed messages from management regarding direction and cause internal bickering and organizational dissonance.

Your Actions: Share the vision and clearly communicate expectations and stay the course.

Don't Like Planning

Not everyone enjoys the focused and detailed work of planning. The lack of attention to detail is rampant. Attention Deficit Disorder is on the rise and has become a major problem for businesses. Instant gratification and impatience lead to a dislike for planning. Many people don't plan to make sure they don't fail.

Your Actions: Reward employees who do-it-right-the-first-time and train employees to plan their work and work their plan.

Lack of Commitment

The level of commitment in general, across the national spectrum, has become questionable. It is difficult for employees to be committed and loyal to a company that has no commitment and loyalty to them—even after decades of service.

Your Actions: Conduct smaller Synergy Team Power Meetings and break down "we" and "them" attitudes by empowering employees to be a part of the solution and success.

Lack of Synergy

This is a leadership-style issue. It's difficult to imagine why some managers think they can order change, teamwork, and trust like they order a pizza. It can't be done!

Your Actions: Communication needs to be clear, constant, and transparent. There is a distinct difference between leadership and management.

Analysis Paralysis

In many cases, over-analysis is based on fear, uncertainty and doubt.

Your Actions: Take control, clearly identify deadlines with a definiteness of purpose. Eliminate excuses and insist on accountability and responsibility.

Power and Control Issues

In organizations that are not accustomed to teamwork, power and control issues are more evident. "If it's not my idea, it doesn't exist" is frequently a blockage to the introduction of new ideas and improvements.

Your Actions: Recognize that power and control are needs for attention and redirect specific talents, energy, and strengths towards positive goals that will satisfy these needs.

Finally . . .

A good strategic plan focuses on integrating people, systems, and structure, thus directing them toward a predetermined, worthwhile vision—a clear set of believable and livable values—and Transformational, Exciting, Authentic, Measurable (TEAM) goals.

The Vision needs to be exciting, challenging, and believable. It needs to build a clear picture of what shared success looks like down the road.

The Values need to be virtuous, such as building relationship trust through personal and professional respect, delivering quality products, and embracing service to one another as well as the customer.

The Goal should focus on achieving the vision, increasing profitability, productivity, and performance with specific and measurable sub-goals.

Systems, Structure, and Functions

A key ingredient for a strategic plan to work is to ensure that systems, job functions, and structure support the vision, values, and goals. Working as a high-performance team and exceeding customer expectations can die very quickly if dictatorial leadership and outdated policies and procedures block positive energy. Of course, all systems, structure, and functions cannot be changed overnight, which is why the Synergy Formula supports the principle of continuous improvement. Thousands of small changes made over time will transform a low-performing outfit into a world-class organization—of that, there is no doubt.

Management Commitment

A steady, consistent commitment and guiding hand is the final component of a successful strategic plan. That means: attending meetings, living the values, embracing the vision, being accountable, and delivering on the goals. By so doing, a leadership magnetism takes hold and energy and effort become authentic and trustworthy. More simply put: Anyone would like to work for a purpose-driven, trustworthy leader who walks the talk.

Real wealth is knowing how to direct energy.
BUCKMINSTER FULLER

Selected Bibliography

Albion, Mark. Making a Life, Making a Living. New York: Warner Books, 2000.

Albrecht, Carl. At America's Service. New York: Warner Books, Inc., 1992.

Alexander, Chris. Creating Extraordinary Joy. Alameda: Hunter House, 2001.

_____. Synergizing Your Business. Lake Forest, CA: 1+1=3 Publishing, 2002.

_____. Joy in the Workplace. Lake Forest, CA: 1+1=3 Publishing, 2003.

Allen, James. As a Man Thinketh. Mount Vernon, NY: The Peter Pauper Press, date not listed.

Autry, James. Real Power. New York: Riverhead Books, 1998.

Barker, Joel Arthur. Paradigms: The Business of Discovering the Future. New York, NY: HarperCollins Publishers, Inc., 1992.

Beatty, Jack. The World According to Peter Drucker. New York: The Free Press, 1998.

Beene, R. Timothy S., Paul F. Nunes, and Walter E. Shill. "The Chief Strategy Officer." Harvard Business Review, October 2007: 84-91.

Bennis, Warren. On Becoming a Leader. Reading, MA: Addison-Wesley Publishing Company, 1989.

Berne, Eric. Games People Play. New York: Grove Press, 1964.

Blanchard, Kenneth and Spencer Johnson. The One Minute Manager. New York: Berkley Books, 1982.

Blanchard, Ken and Sheldon Bowles. Gung Ho! New York: William Morrow and Company, Inc., 1998.

Blanchard, Ken, Jim Ballard, and Fred Finch. Customer Mania! New York: Simon & Schuster, Inc., 2004.

Bonstingl, John Jay. Schools of Quality. Thousand Oaks, CA: Corwin Press, Inc., 2001.

Borysenko, Joan and Miroslav. The Power of the Mind to Heal. Carlsbad, CA: Hay House, 1996.

Bossidy, Larry and Ram Charan. Execution. New York: Crown Business, 2002.

Bower, Joseph L. and Clark G. Gilbert. "How Managers' Everyday Decisions Create - or Destroy - Your Company's Strategy." Harvard Business Review,February 2007: 72-79.

Bruce, Anne and James S. Pepitone. Motivating Employees. Madison, WI. McGraw-Hill, 1999.

Buscaglia, Leo F. Living, Loving & Learning. New York: Ballantine Books, 1983.

Butler, Gillian and Tony Hope. Managing Your Mind. New York: Oxford University Press, 1995.

Byham, William C. Zapp! The Lighting of Empowerment. New York: Ballantine Books, 1988.

Capodagli, Bill and Lynn Jackson. The Disney Way. New York: McGraw-Hill, 1999.

Charan, Ram. Know-How. New York. Random House, Inc., 2007.

Christensen, Clayton M., Stephen P. Kaufman, and Willy C. Shih. "Innovation Killers: How Financial Tools Destroy Your Capacity to Do New Things." Harvard Business Review - Leadership & Strategy for the Twenty-first Century, January 2008: 98-105.

Collins, James C. and Jerry I. Porras. Built to Last. New York: HarperCollins Publishers Inc., 1994.

Collins, Jim. Good to Great. New York: HarperCollins Publishers Inc., 2001.

Covey, Stephen R. The 7 Habits of Highly Effective People. New York: Simon & Schuster, Inc., 1990.

_____. Principle-Centered Leadership. New York: Simon & Schuster, Inc., 1992.

Dell, Chip R. Managers as Mentors. San Francisco, CA: Berrett-Koehler Publishers, Inc., 1996.

DeLong, Thomas J., John J. Gabarro, and Robert J. Lees. "Why Mentoring Matters in a Hypercompetitive World." Harvard Business Review - Leadership & Strategy for the Twenty-first Century, January 2008: 115-121.

Denove, Chris and James D. Power IV. <u>Satisfaction</u>. New York: Penguin Group, 2006.

De Pree, Max. <u>Leadership Jazz</u>. New York: Dell Publishing, 1993.

DeVos, Rich. <u>Compassionate Capitalism</u>. New York: Penguin Group, 1994.

Dodd, Dominic and Ken Favaro. "Managing the Right Tension." <u>Harvard Business Review</u>, December 2006: 62-74.

Dotlich, David L. and Peter C. Cairo. <u>Action Coaching</u>. San Francisco, CA: Jossey-Bass Publishers, 1999.

Drucker, Peter F. <u>The New Realities</u>. New York: Harper and Row Publishers, 1989.

_____. <u>The Effective Executive</u>. New York: Harper and Row Publishers, 1996.

_____. <u>Management Challenges for the Twenty First Century</u>. New York: HarperCollins Publishers Inc., 1999.

Elkin, Allen. <u>Stress Management for Dummies</u>. Foster City, CA: IDG Books Worldwide, Inc., 1999.

Freiberg, Kevin and Jackie. <u>Nuts! Southwest Airlines' Crazy Recipe for Business and Personal Success.</u> Austin, TX: Bard Press, 1996.

Fuller, R. Buckminster. <u>Synergetics-Explorations in the Geometry of Thinking</u>. New York: MacMillan Publishers, 1975.

Gallo, Fred P. <u>Energy Psychology</u>. Boca Raton, FL: CRC Press, 1999.

Gardner, Howard. "The Ethical Mind." <u>Harvard Business Review</u>, March 2007: 51-56.

Gerber, Michael. <u>The E-Myth Manager</u>. New York: HarperCollins Publishers Inc., 1998.

Goffee, Rob and Gareth Jones. "Leading Clever People." <u>Harvard Business Review</u>, March 2007: 72-79.

Goleman, Daniel. <u>Emotional Intelligence</u>. New York: Bantam Books, 1995.

Goleman, Daniel, Richard Boyatzis, and Annie McKee. <u>Primal Leadership: Learning to Lead with Emotional Intelligence</u>. Boston, MA: Harvard Business School, 2002.

Greenleaf, Robert K. <u>On Becoming a Servant Leader</u>. Edited by Frick, Don M. and Spears, Larry C. San Francisco, CA: Jossey-Bass Publishers, 1996.

Greiner, Donna and Kinni, Theodore B. <u>1,001 Ways to Keep Customers Coming Back</u>. Rocklin, CA: Prima Publishing, 1999.

Hammer, Kay. <u>Workplace Warrior</u>. New York: AMA Publications, 2000.

Handy, Charles. <u>The Hungry Spirit</u>. New York: Bantam Doubleday Dell Publishing Groups, Inc., 1998.

Hawkins, David R. <u>Power vs. Force</u>. Carlsbad, CA: Hay House, Inc., 2002.

Henricks, Mark. <u>Grow Your Business</u>. Irvine, CA: Entrepreneur Press, 2001.

Hill, Linda A. "Where Will We Find Tomorrow's Leaders?" <u>Harvard Business Review - Leadership & Strategy for the Twenty-first Century</u>, January 2008: 123-129.

Hill, Napoleon. <u>Think and Grow Rich</u>. North Hollywood, CA: Wilshire Book Company, 1966.

_____. <u>Law of Success</u>. Chicago, IL: Success Unlimited, Inc., 1979.

Hogan, Eve Eschner, with Steven Hogan. <u>Intellectual Foreplay</u>. Alameda, CA: Hunter House, 2000.

Holmes, Ernest. <u>The Science of Mind</u>. New York: Dodd, Mead, and Company, 1938.

Jampolsky, Gerald. <u>Love is Letting Go of Fear</u>. Berkeley, CA: Celestial Arts, 1979.

John Paul II, His Holiness. <u>Crossing the Threshold of Hope</u>. New York: Random House, 1994.

Kanter, Rosabeth Moss. "Transforming Giants." <u>Harvard Business Review - Leadership & Strategy for the Twenty-first Century</u>, January 2008: 43-52.

Kaplan, Robert S. and David P. Norton. "Mastering the Management System." <u>Harvard Business Review - Leadership & Strategy for the Twenty-first Century</u>, January 2008: 62-77.

Katzenbach, Jon R. and Douglas K. Smith. The Wisdom of Teams. New York: Harvard Business School Press, 1993.

Kouzes, James M. and Barry Z. Posner. The Leadership Challenge. San Francisco, CA: Jossey-Bass Publishers, 1995.

Krieger, Robert J. and Louis Patler. If it ain't broke...Break it! New York: Warner Books, Inc., 1991.

Leadership . . . with a Human Touch. Jan 18, 1994; May 10, 1994; May 9, 1995; June 6, 1995. Economics Press, Inc., Fairfield, NJ.

Lencioni, Patrick. The Five Dysfunctions of a Team, San Francisco, CA: Jossey-Bass Publishers, 2002.

Lindbergh, Anne Morrow. Gifts from the Sea. New York: Pantheon Book, Inc., 1955.

Loehr, Jim and Tony Schwartz. The Power of Full Engagement. New York: Free Press, 2003.

Logan, Dave, John King, and Halee Fischer-Wright. Tribal Leadership. New York: HarperCollins Publishers Inc., 2008.

Maltz, Maxwell. Psycho-Cybernetics. Hollywood, CA: Wilshire Book Company, 1965.

Mandino, Og. The Greatest Salesman in the World. New York: Bantam Books, 1968.

_____. The Greatest Miracle in the World. New York: Bantam Books, 1975.

_____. The Greatest Salesman in the World, Part II, New York: Bantam Books, 1988.

Mann, Nancy R. The Keys to Excellence. The Deming Philosophy. London, England: Mercury Books, 1989.

Marriott, J.W. Jr. and Kathi Ann Brown. The Spirit to Serve. New York: HarperCollins Publishers, Inc., 1997.

Martin, Roger. "How Successful Leaders Think." Harvard Business Review, June 2007: 60-67.

McBryde, Linda. The Mass Market Woman. Eagle River, Alaska: Crowded Hour Press, 1999.

McWilliams, John-Roger and Peter McWilliams. <u>Life 101: You Can't Afford the Luxury of a Negative Thought.</u> Los Angeles, CA: Prelude Press, 1988.

———. <u>Life 101</u>. Los Angeles, CA: Prelude Press, 1991.

Medina, John J. "The Science of Thinking Smarter." <u>Harvard Business Review</u>, May 2008: 51-54.

Montgomery, Cynthia A. "Putting Leadership Back into Strategy." <u>Harvard Business Review - Leadership & Strategy for the Twenty-first Century</u>, January 2008: 54-60.

Montrose, Philip. <u>Getting through to Your Emotions with EFT</u>. Sacramento, CA: Holistic Communications, 2000.

Moore, Thomas. <u>Original Self</u>. New York: HarperCollins Publishers Inc., 1981.

Neidert, David. <u>Four Seasons of Leadership</u>. Provo, UT: Executive Excellence Publishing, 1999.

Nerburn, Kent and Louise Mengelkoch. <u>Native American Wisdom</u>. San Rafael, CA: New World Library, 1991.

Nerburn, Kent. <u>The Soul of an Indian</u>. San Rafael, CA: New World Library, 1993.

Novak, Philip. <u>The World's Wisdom</u>. Edison, NJ: Castle Books, 1996.

Ornish, Dean. <u>Love and Survival: The Scientific Basis for the Healing Power of Intimacy</u>. New York: HarperCollins Publishers Inc., 1998.

Palmer, Parker J. <u>Active Life</u>. San Francisco, CA: Jossey-Bass Publishers, 1990.

———. <u>Let your Life Speak</u>. San Francisco, CA: Jossey-Bass Publishers, 2000.

Pearsall, Paul. <u>The Pleasure Prescription</u>. Alameda, CA: Hunter House, 1998.

Peck, M. Scott. <u>The Road Less Traveled</u>. New York: Simon & Schuster, Inc., 1978.

Pert, Candace and Deepak Chopra. <u>Molecules of Emotion</u>. New York: Scribner, 1997.

Peters, Thomas J. and Robert H. Waterman, Jr. <u>In Search of Excellence</u>. New York: Warner Books, 1982.

_____. <u>Thriving on Chaos</u>. New York: Harper Perennial, 1987.

_____. <u>Liberation Management</u>. New York: Alfred A. Knopf, 1992.

Plunket, Warren R., Raymond F. Attner, and Gemmy S. Allen. <u>Management: Meeting and Exceeding Customer Expectation</u>, 8th Edition. Mason: Thompson South-Western, 2005.

Porter, Michael E. "The Five Competitive Forces That Shape Strategy." <u>Harvard Business Review - Leadership & Strategy for the Twenty-first Century</u>, January 2008: 78-93.

Robbins, Anthony. <u>Awaken the Giant Within</u>. New York: Summit Books, 1991.

Russell, Peter. <u>The Brain Book</u>. New York: Penguin Group, 1979.

Schein, Edgar H. <u>Organizational Culture and Leadership</u>. San Francisco, CA: Jossey-Bass, 2004.

Senge, Peter M. <u>The Fifth Discipline.</u> New York: DoubleDay, 1994.

Simon, David. <u>Vital Energy</u>. New York: Wiley, 2000.

Slone, Reuben E., John T. Meltzer, and J. Paul Dittman. "Are You the Weakest Link in Your Company's Supply Chain?" <u>Harvard Business Review</u>, September 2007: 116-127.

Spector, Robert and Patrick D. McCarthy. <u>The Nordstrom's Way: The Inside Story of America's # 1 Customer Service Company</u>. New York: John Wiley and Sons, Inc., 1995.

Spitzer, Robert J. <u>The Spirit of Leadership</u>. Provo, UT: Executive Excellence Publishing, 2000.

Stanley, Andy. <u>Visioneering</u>. Sisters, OR: Multnomah Publishers, Inc., 1999.

Star, Jonathan. <u>Rumi</u>. New York: Penguin Putnam Inc., 1997.

Staub, Robert E. II. <u>The Acts of Courage</u>. Provo, UT: Executive Excellence Publishing, 1999.

Stevenson, Howard H. "How to Change the World." <u>Harvard Business Review - Leadership & Strategy for the Twenty-first Century</u>, January 2008: 29-33.

Steward, Marjabelle Young and Marian Faux. <u>Executive Etiquette in the New Workplace</u>. New York: St. Martin's Press, 1994.

Thomas, R. David. <u>Dave's Way</u>. New York: Berkley Books, 1992.

Thompson, G. Liam. <u>E-Business to Go</u>. St. Louis, MO: Appollaso Publishing, 2001.

Thoreau, Henry David. <u>Walden and Other Writings</u>. New York: Barnes & Noble Books, 1993.

Tracy, Brian. <u>The 100 Absolutely Unbreakable Laws of Business Success</u>. San Francisco, CA: Berrett-Koehler Publishers, Inc., 2000.

_____. <u>Advance Selling Strategies</u>. New York: Simon & Schuster, Inc., 1995.

Trimble, Vance H. <u>Sam Walton, Founder of Walmart</u>. New York: Penguin Books, 1990. Ward, Andrew J. et al. "Improving the Performance of Top Management Teams." <u>MIT Sloan Management Review</u>, Spring 2007: 85-90.

Wasserstein, Bruce. "The HBR Interview: Giving Great Advice." <u>Harvard Business Review - Leadership & Strategy for the Twenty-first Century</u>, January 2008: 106-113.

Welch, Jack. <u>Jack, Straight from the Gut</u>. New York: Warner Books, Inc., 2001.

_____. <u>Winning</u>. New York: HarperCollins Publishers Inc., 2005.

Wheatley, Margaret J. and Myron Kellner-Rogers, <u>A Simpler Way</u>. San Francisco, CA: Berrett-Koehler, 1996.

Wolf, Fred Alan. <u>Mind into Matter</u>. Portsmouth, NH: Moment Point Press, 2001.

Ziff, Lazer. <u>Ralph Waldo Emerson - Selected Essays</u>. New York: Penguin Books, 1984.

Zingheim, Patricia K. and J.R. Schuster. <u>Pay People Right</u>. San Francisco, CA: Jossey-Bass Publishers, 2000.

Zukav, Gary. <u>The Seat of the Soul.</u> New York: Fireside, 1989.

Synergizing Your Business

The 5 Essential Pieces for High-Performance—A Series of Business Books

by Chris Alexander

The 5 Essential Pieces

2. Strategic Planning Retreats

3. Leadership Skills Workshops

1. TEAM POWER RETREAT

5. Customized Sales Workshops

4. Customer Care Workshops

Teamwork divides the task and doubles the success.

Synergizing Your Business

The 5 Essential Pieces for High-Performance

The Synergy Formula, 1+1=3, energizes the people in your business to effectively work as a high-performance team. We are experts at getting an entire organization to "play from the same sheet of music." Our formula improves communication, builds trust, and empowers individuals with a sense of purpose. We motivate everyone into taking greater responsibility and accountability for their jobs. When employees have a say in the things that affect them, they willingly give their best efforts and produce more, reduce costs, and ultimately "WOW" customers.

Synergy workshops and seminars build relationship trust and break through walls of negativity and resistance, thus allowing for the essential pieces for collaboration between management and employees to strengthen. The essential pieces of collaboration are vision ownership; core values; teamwork; "WOW" factor goals; and a clearly defined, shared destiny. When the motivational puzzle snaps together, a greater sense of belonging and a culture of emotional security are formed, resulting in a strong foundation for high-performance teamwork.

A major benefit within the Synergy Formula is our experience and ability to instantly tap into and direct the human energy source of a business. We have proven in company after company and industry after industry that harnessing human potential and energy, and directing it toward a shared destiny, multiplies the potential for success. We know how to create unstoppable, unflappable, and unshakable zones of inspiration, and secure highly profitable businesses. We focus on building shared responsibility, strong relationships, shared values, shared goals, and collective spiritual agreements—all sources of inspiration and energy. The outcome? The greatest competitive advantage a business can possess: A team of professionals committed to "WOWING" customers.

Essential Piece #1: Synergy Team Power – The 5 Success Habits of High-Performance Business Teams

Synergy Team Power is the foundation of the Synergy Formula and has proven to be successful in many companies and industries worldwide. When an organization comes together and is united behind a common set of goals and core values, the potential for extraordinary achievement is unlimited and without boundaries.

High-performance business teams need structured, ongoing coaching, nurturing, development, and discipline. Discipline is the bedfellow of teamwork and improves the quality of workmanship across the board. Training, education, good systems, and structure are fundamental to making your team world-class. The synergy magic happens through the team's combined effort and commitment to practice a given set of core values.

Practicing core values and insisting that core values become a platform for decision-making will teach employees how to build relationship trust, loyalty, commitment, and respect. The environment and climate play a major role in marshaling the collective brainpower and creative energy of your team. Therein lies the true source of power.

Essential Piece #2: Synergy Strategic Planning - A Blueprint for Organizational Planning and Execution

A good strategic plan focuses on integrating people, systems, and structure, thus directing them toward a predetermined, worthwhile vision—a clear set of believable and livable values—and Transformational, Exciting, Authentic, Measurable (TEAM) goals.

The Vision needs to be exciting, challenging, and believable. It needs to build a clear picture of what shared success looks like down the road.

The Values need to be virtuous, such as building relationship trust through personal and professional respect, delivering quality products, and embracing service to one another as well as the customer.

The Goal should focus on achieving the vision, increasing profitability, productivity, and performance with specific and measurable sub-goals.

Real wealth is knowing how to direct energy.

BUCKMINSTER FULLER

Systems, Structure, and Functions

A key ingredient for a strategic plan to work is to ensure that systems, job functions, and structure support the vision, values, and goals. Working as a high-performance team and exceeding customer expectations can die very quickly if dictatorial leadership and outdated policies and procedures block positive energy. Of course, all systems, structure, and functions cannot be changed overnight, which is why the Synergy Formula supports the principle of continuous improvement. Thousands of small changes made over time will transform a low-performing outfit into a world-class organization—of that, there is no doubt.

Management Commitment

A steady, consistent commitment and guiding hand is the final component of a successful strategic plan. That means: attending meetings, living the values, embracing the vision, being accountable, and delivering on the goals. By so doing, a leadership magnetism takes hold and energy and effort become authentic and trustworthy. More simply put: Anyone would like to work for a purpose-driven, trustworthy leader who walks the talk.

What gets measured gets done.

Essential Piece #3: Synergy Leadership— The Art and Practice of Building and Leading High-Performance Business Teams

Synergy Leaders are the communicators and motivators of the vision, values, and goals, initiating communication and building relationship trust. It is their responsibility to coach, counsel, and mentor individuals through the process of organizational change. They build high-performance teamwork through daily practical behavioral application. From the CEO to the frontline manager, the integrity of the entire business depends upon whether the executive team practices good leadership principles and become the examples and catalysts for positive change.

When the leadership team is on the same page, the rest of the organization falls more easily into alignment. Understanding how to practice an accepted strong set of leadership behavioral skills creates a greater sense of competency in an employee's mind, particularly if the core values are seen to be practiced and supported. An attitudinal and loyalty synergy "glue" is then created between management and staff.

We have all worked for companies that are confused about their leadership style. Unity of direction, leadership, and consistent role modeling are critical components for success. They demonstrate that we are truly dedicated to building a culture of integrity.

Essential Piece #4: The "WOW" Factor!— How to Bring The "WOW" Factor! into Your Business and Earn Customer Loyalty for Life

The "WOW" Factor! begins with treating everyone you work with as your customer. It incorporates the Golden Rule: "Treat others as you would like to be treated." Therefore, customer service is a worthy business core value, as well as an important personal one. Employees tend to treat customers as they are treated by the company. Bad service and bad attitudes are merely reflections of the way people have become accustomed to treating one another.

Since synergy works from the "inside out," it's paramount that everyone in every department understands the principle of service. Service from the internal to the external drives the financial engine of a business. Good service increases revenue, lowers costs, and reduces staff attrition. Everyone should be service minded and empowered to solve problems immediately and directly. The senior executives, managers, service representatives, salespeople, and receptionists need to be committed to service. Trust and loyalty are reinforced when all customers are taken care of in an effective, efficient, and friendly manner.

Essential Piece #5: Synergy Sales Power— The Art and Skill of Relationship Selling

Synergy Sales Power focuses on the importance of building long-term, quality relationships with customers. As a part of the Synergy Process, Sales Power focuses on building a solid reputation of trust by assisting the customer in establishing his/her true needs and wants.

Synergy focuses on *relationship selling* and building customers for life. Relationships are formed between people before contracts are signed.

Customers will act on recommendations from salespeople they trust. Synergy relationship selling is based on understanding a customer's buying style and adapting to it, thus building trust that leads to increased sales, referrals, low-cost customer retention, and happy and loyal customers.

By synergizing with your customer, you are able to build highly-profitable, triple-win relationships.

Chris Alexander M.A. (Org. Psych.)
Professional Speaker, Award-Winning Business-Building Strategist, and Author

If you would like to hear the words: World-Class!, Outstanding!, Impressive!, and Inspiring!, then book Chris Alexander to speak at your next meeting.

Because of Chris Alexander's books, powerful messages, and engaging humorous teaching gift, businesses and organizations throughout the world invite him to speak and coach their executives and business teams.

Executives from client companies such as Barratt American, Mercedes Benz, Interior Specialists, Inc., and Johnson & Johnson say that it is Alexander's 30 years of real world business experience, examples, and results that have struck a chord with them and won him acclaim.

Alexander is an expert at building organizational culture, high-performance teamwork, and world-class customer service. He conducts Synergy retreats, custom designed workshops, and ongoing culture change programs.

Alexander's speaking topics include:

- Synergy Strategic Planning
- World-Class Leadership
- The "WOW" Factor!
- Synergy Team Power
- Synergy Sales Power
- Synergy Communication Styles

He says: "Synergy is about those magic moments—when working in concert toward a shared destiny—communication flows openly, and everyone feels a sense of belonging and connection. That synchronicity multiplies, energy, focus, fun, and productivity. We see it in sports teams and in business teams—there's no difference."

Chris Alexander is an example of the American dream: He was born in a small country in the middle of Africa, then called Rhodesia and now renamed Zimbabwe. He emigrated from Africa to the U.S. 20 years ago and is the author of *Catch the Wind with Your Wings, Creating Extraordinary Joy, Joy in the Workplace*, and *Synergizing Your Business*—a series of 5 business books.

He has also authored many successful business audios, CDs, and DVDs to support his training programs. Along with a team of educational specialists, Alexander won the prestigious Los Angeles Area Emmy Award for Overall Excellence in Business Education for the Coast Telecourse, Dollar$ and Sense: Personal Finance for the 21st Century. Alexander's largest audience is his two PBS TV shows, titled "Creating Extraordinary Joy" and "Joy in the Workplace," which reaches 4.5 million people with each broadcast.

Alexander's stories, anecdotes, international flavor, and fresh feet-on-the-ground examples will "WOW" your audiences . . . and like so many groups, you will want him to come back—again and again.

For more information:

SynergyTeamPower.com

AlexanderSpeaks.com

ChrisAlexanderBooks.com

(U.S.) 949/586-0511

CAlexander@SynergyTeamPower.com

*I am enough of an artist to draw
fully on my imagination.
Imagination is more important
than knowledge.
Knowledge is limited.
Imagination encircles the world.*

ALBERT EINSTEIN

www.ingramcontent.com/pod-product-compliance
Lightning Source LLC
Chambersburg PA
CBHW060603210326
41519CB00014B/3557